Organizational Culture

Organizational Culture

A Guide to Inclusive Transformation

Marie Carasco

KoganPage

Publisher's note

Every possible effort has been made to ensure that the information contained in this book is accurate at the time of going to press, and the publishers and author cannot accept responsibility for any errors or omissions, however caused. No responsibility for loss or damage occasioned to any person acting, or refraining from action, as a result of the material in this publication can be accepted by the editor, the publisher or the author.

First published in Great Britain and the United States in 2024 by Kogan Page Limited

2nd Floor, 45 Gee Street
London
EC1V 3RS
United Kingdom

8 W 38th Street, Suite 902
New York, NY 10018
USA

www.koganpage.com

Kogan Page books are printed on paper from sustainable forests.

ISBNs

Hardback   978 1 3986 1502 1
Paperback   978 1 3986 1499 4
Ebook   978 1 3986 1500 7

British Library Cataloguing-in-Publication Data
A CIP record for this book is available from the British Library.

Library of Congress Cataloging-in-Publication Data
Names: Carasco, Marie, author.
Title: Organizational culture : a guide to inclusive transformation / Marie
  Carasco.
Description: London ; New York, NY : Kogan Page Inc., 2024. | Includes
  bibliographical references and index.
Identifiers: LCCN 2024009613 (print) | LCCN 2024009614 (ebook) | ISBN
  9781398614994 (pbk) | ISBN 9781398615021 (hbk) | ISBN 9781398615007
  (ebk)
Subjects: LCSH: Corporate culture. | Organizational behavior. | Diversity
  in the workplace.
Classification: LCC HD58.7 .C3478 2024 (print) | LCC HD58.7 (ebook) | DDC
  658.3–dc23/eng/20240318
LC record available at https://lccn.loc.gov/2024009613
LC ebook record available at https://lccn.loc.gov/2024009614

Typeset by Integra Software Services, Pondicherry
Print production managed by Jellyfish
Printed and bound by CPI Group (UK) Ltd, Croydon, CR0 4YY

*For
De Abreu
DiAngelo and Evelyn
No matter the outcome, it was, is and
always will be
sufficiently sufficient.*

CONTENTS

About the Author x
About the Field of Organization Development xii
Acknowledgments xviii

Introduction 1

1 A Holistic Framework for Transforming Organizational Culture 5

Understand Psychological Contracts 5
Establish Psychological Safety 9
Cultivate Cross-Company Partnerships 12
Leverage Employee Engagement for Sustained
    Implementation 15
References 17

2 The Role of Employee Engagement in Socially Impactful Initiatives 19

The History of Corporate Social Responsibility 19
Motivation and Engagement 21
Engaging Employees in Social Change Initiatives 26
The Impact of the Covid-19 Pandemic 33
Organizations Leveraging Social Impact Initiatives Across
    Industries 35
References 41

3 Employees as Advocates of Equity-based Initiatives 43

Defining Diversity, Equity, Inclusion, and Belonging 43
The Importance of DEIB Initiatives in Organizations 44

The Role of Employees as DEIB Advocates 45
The Impact of DEIB Initiatives on Organizational Success 45
References 56

4 Psychological Contracts 59

Unpacking Unspoken Employee Expectations 61
Summary 76
References 78

5 Psychological Safety 81

Benefits of Psychological Safety 89
Creating Psychological Safety 90
Psychological Safety and Organization Culture Change 92
Other Considerations 95
References 96

6 Supporting Employees as Catalysts 99

Influencing Influencers 101
Understanding the Types of Change 103
Communication 105
The Role and Significance of Employee Engagement 106
References 115

7 Partnerships Needed for Achieving Culture Transformation 119

Stakeholder Identification 121
Partnerships Needed by Levels in the Organization 122
Partnerships Needed by Business Unit 126
Examples of Internal Partnerships 130
External Partnerships to Consider 131
Partnership with Yourself 133
References 136

8 **Elevating the Significance of Employee Resource Groups** 139

A Brief History of ERGs 139
Some Reasons Why Diversity Initiatives Fail 144
ERGs as Strategic Partners 149
Leader Commitment, Buy-in, and Accountability 155
References 158

9 **Bringing It All Together** 161

An Interview Between Marie Carasco and Jaison Williams 161

Index 189

ABOUT THE AUTHOR

Marie Carasco PhD, MBA, GPHR, SHRM-SCP is the founder and chief social scientist of Talent en Floré LLC, a female-led, black-owned executive coaching and organization change consulting practice supporting those interested in being better leaders, clarifying purpose or with a desire for change (see www.talentenflore.com). At the time of this publication, she is Vice President, Organization Development, Culture & Diversity at GitHub, and General Manager/Partner, Organization Development, Culture & Diversity at Microsoft. As an inclusive change agent, she has served as a trusted advisor to c-level leadership teams managing taskforces for large-scale global change initiatives, human resources strategy, and applied research initiatives in multiple sectors.

Marie is an International Coaching Federation Professional Certified Coach (PCC) and has deep functional expertise in high-potential leader development and appreciative approaches to managing change. Her work uses multiple interventions that connect workplace psychology principles to business and organization challenges. She has taught graduate-level courses in Organizational Behavior, Organization Development, Global Diversity, Group Processes, and Leadership Studies at George Mason University, City University of New York–Brooklyn College, and Azusa Pacific University, and she was also a practice supervisor/subject matter expert and mentor at Concordia University in Montréal, Québec, Canada. Her research and professional interests are in leader development, identity and belonging, organization development (OD) competencies, culture cultivation, and qualitative research methods.

Marie holds a PhD in Workforce Education and Development with an emphasis in Human Resource Development and Organization Development from Penn State University and an MBA in Organizational Behavior and Coaching from the University of Texas at Dallas, Naveen Jindal School of Management. She also holds an undergraduate degree in psychology and a graduate degree in industrial-organizational psychology from CUNY-Brooklyn College.

She is the co-author of *The Essential HR Guide for Small Businesses and Start-ups* (Society for Human Resource Management, 2020) and has authored book chapters in *Rethinking Organizational Diversity, Equity, and Inclusion: A Step-by-Step Guide for Facilitating Effective Change* (Taylor & Francis Group, 2022), *Organization Development (OD) Interventions: Executing Effective Organizational Change* (Productivity Press Taylor & Francis Group, 2021), *Evaluating Organization Development: How to Ensure and Sustain the Successful Transformation* (CRC Press, 2017), and *Marketing Organization Development Consulting: A How-To Guide for OD Consultants* (CRC Press, 2017). She has also published articles including "The Challenges That Come When Doing Organization Development Work" (*Eye on Psi Chi*, April 2022), "Leveraging Applied Behavioral Science in Business Settings: The Field of Organization Development" (*Eye on Psi Chi*, November 2021), and "Leadership and Employee Engagement: Proposing Research Agendas through a Review of Literature" (*Human Resource Development Review*, 2014). You can reach her at marie@talentenflore.com.

ABOUT THE FIELD OF ORGANIZATION DEVELOPMENT

The goal of the field of organization development (OD) is culture transformation that is achieved through deliberate planned change interventions rooted in behavioral science. In layman's terms, OD can help to drive change at all levels in an organization system (individual level, group, team, and company-wide), to help align strategy, improve leadership effectiveness, and even drive culture change.

Some Historical Context

Organizations having to adapt to an ever-changing business environment gave rise to the field of organization development in the 1940s and 1950s. Numerous academic fields, including psychology, sociology, and anthropology, influenced OD, and the field was significantly shaped by pioneers like Douglas McGregor, Edgar Schein, and Kurt Lewin. The origins of organizational dynamics can be seen in the mid-20th century; after World War II, technology advanced quickly and became more complicated, making old, inflexible architecture outdated. Leaders such as Kurt Lewin, Elton Mayo, and Chris Argyris saw that a new strategy was required, one that put equal emphasis on the human elements that drive organizational success as well as efficiency. Initially referred to as "group dynamics" or "organizational behavior," this emerging topic served as a precursor to what would eventually be recognized as OD.

OD consultants and practitioners became more and more prevalent in the 1960s and 1970s as organizations struggled with fast industrialization and societal changes. A well-known figure in this era,

Warner Burke, promoted an action-oriented strategy that prioritized teamwork, data-driven interventions, and ongoing learning. Burke's planned change paradigm, which prioritizes diagnosis, action, and evaluation, served as a blueprint for many practitioners. In addition to Burke, individuals such as Edgar Schein, Richard Beckhard, and David Nadler offered their distinct viewpoints, influencing the varied fabric of techniques in OD.

The last several decades have seen additional changes. Organizations now need to be even more agile and adaptable due to factors including globalization, technological upheavals, and the growth of knowledge economies. OD welcomed this changing environment and broadened its offering beyond conventional training and team-building initiatives. Approaches like complexity theory and strategic change management gained appeal alongside appreciative inquiry, which focuses on organizational accomplishments and strengths. The emphasis changed from "solving issues" to "making lasting transformations," with a focus on systemic change and individual empowerment.

Types of Interventions

OD professionals use a range of approaches to help organizations support change. There are four primary types of intervention: interventions pertaining to human processes, strategic, technological/structural, and human resource management. Enhancing interpersonal connections, team dynamics, and communication are the main goals of human process interventions. Techno-structural interventions refer to modifications made to technology and organizational systems. Aligning organizational goals and strategies is the goal of strategic interventions. Interventions in human resource management are aimed at improving the motivation and growth of employees. Similar to adept navigators, OD practitioners use a wide range of instruments to negotiate the choppy waters of transition. Focus groups, interviews, and survey questions are useful tools for identifying hidden problems and diagnosing organizational dynamics. Team-building activities encourage cooperation and communication, while leadership development courses give participants the tools they need to help their teams through change. Large-group interventions and strategic planning sessions help groups work together more successfully, while process consultation (anchored in group observation and feedback) supports group goal-setting and collective visioning. When used sensitively and expertly, these approaches give businesses the ability to choose their own path to success.

Major Contributors to the Field

OD has benefited from the wisdom of a multitude of contributors. Warner Burke is still regarded as a pioneer in the field because of his focus on data-driven transformation, and has aided in the knowledge of group dynamics. His work on the "Burke-Litwin Model" has provided a framework for diagnosing and understanding organizational change. Edgar Schein's research on corporate culture is still a valuable resource for practitioners seeking to comprehend the unseen factors influencing human conduct. Richard Beckhard's change model offered a guide for managing transformation, and David Nadler provided frameworks for organizational design. Douglas McGregor, who suggested Theory X and Theory Y as contrasting management philosophies, is another important contributor. These and countless others have had a lasting impression on the discipline, serving as role models and inspiration for future generations of OD practitioners.

Challenges in Doing OD Work

OD comes with several challenges. I've discovered that occasionally, despite best efforts, business moves more quickly than intended, leaving people out. One reason could be that including some groups raises more queries and viewpoints, which would delay the completion of a desired activity or decision-making process. While moving quickly can boost productivity, there is a price paid with things like attrition, employee resistance to changes, and poor employee engagement. Dissonance and low morale can arise when workers are left out of experiences and activities that they feel they should be a part of. At worst, this can result in workers becoming disruptive or unhelpful during a change effort or potentially leaving the firm (Carasco, 2022).

Establishing trust and using effective communication strategies are essential for overcoming reluctance. Another challenge that comes with doing OD work is the difficulty in pinpointing the underlying causes of problems and the process of creating effective ways of addressing them. Like many other roles in a company, to execute successful change projects, OD practitioners also need to manage organizational politics and power dynamics.

Controversies in Organization Development

Throughout its history, OD has encountered ethical disputes and implementation difficulties. The application of personality tests in business settings, as a part of development and selection is one area of disagreement. Opponents contend that these evaluations have the potential to reinforce prejudice and restrict chances for people of color. Large-group interventions have also drawn criticism for their propensity to subjugate individual agency and control emotions. Furthermore, stringent ethical rules and open communication with all stakeholders are necessary to ensure data privacy and confidentiality during interventions.

Critics of the field have questioned its scientific rigor, pointing out that determining the impact of interventions can be challenging. Several issues have been brought up, including the possibility of power disparities between consultants and clients and the danger of forcing "one-size-fits-all" solutions on a variety of organizational settings. Other disagreements have surfaced over the years, including the usefulness of OD interventions as one of the points of contention.

Opponents claim that it is hard to gauge the success of OD interventions and that there is scant empirical data to support them. The function of OD practitioners is the subject of another debate, with some contending that practitioners might cross lines and impede an organization's right to autonomy. Rebuilding the field's reputation and confidence requires confronting these issues head-on and adhering to the strictest ethical guidelines.

Becoming an OD Practitioner

A combination of practical skills and academic understanding is needed to become an OD practitioner. Graduate programs in the field are widely available at institutions, giving students a strong foundation in group dynamics, change management, and research methodologies. One can further improve credibility in the industry by earning certifications from associations such as the International Society for Organization Development and Change (ISODC) or the Organization Development Network (ODN).

A solid foundation can be obtained with master's degrees in organization behavior, organization development, or comparable disciplines like organizational psychology. Furthermore, developing practical experience through internships or entry-level jobs with internal OD departments, HR teams, or consulting firms helps to refine understanding and creates a strong portfolio. It is still necessary to engage in ongoing education through conferences, workshops, and professional development initiatives in order to stay current with the rapidly changing field, and let's not forget the importance of "working on your stuff" through personal development.

The Future of OD

As we stand at the precipice of a future teeming with uncertainty and disruption, the need for effective OD practices has never been greater. Organizations desperately need guidance in navigating rapid technological advancements, the ever-evolving talent landscape, and the increasing demands for sustainability and social responsibility. The future of OD is bright, with exciting possibilities on the horizon. Embracing technology offers new avenues for data collection, analysis, and intervention delivery. Exploring the neuroscience of organizational behavior promises deeper insights into human decision-making and motivation. Venturing into new domains like sustainability and social impact can help organizations contribute to a more just and equitable future. By staying attuned to emerging trends, remaining adaptable, and upholding the highest ethical standards, OD practitioners can continue to serve as vital navigators, guiding organizations toward transformation and long-term success.

From its modest origins in the postwar era to its changing position in the modern world, organization development has demonstrated its worth as a crucial field that supports learning, helps companies navigate change, and ultimately leads them to a prosperous future. OD professionals may navigate the choppy waters of organizational transformation with confidence if they have a wide range of tools at their disposal, a steadfast dedication to moral behavior, and a sharp eye for new opportunities. By using a variety of strategies, OD professionals aim to enhance organizational performance and encourage positive transformation, and so the value and importance of OD's involvement increases. Advances in technology and shifting social norms are calling on OD skills to navigate change, and OD practitioners are in a good position to lead organizations through these challenging times because of their knowledge of human dynamics. Future developments in OD include embracing technology, delving into the neurology of organizational behavior, and connecting more deliberately with social impact, as this book proposes.

Reference

Carasco, M. (2022). The challenges that come when doing organization development work. *Eye on Psi Chi Magazine*, https://www.psichi.org/page/264Eye Summer22Carasco (archived at https://perma.cc/9PM8-8Z8E)

ACKNOWLEDGMENTS

This book would have never come to fruition had it not been for my serendipitous meeting of Bronwyn Geyer, who at the time was an acquisitions editor at Kogan Page. I'm grateful to you and the publisher for providing me with this wonderful opportunity to share my experience and perspectives in this solo publication.

I also want to acknowledge and thank Joe Ferner-Reeves, my editor at Kogan Page, for an excellent collaborative experience.

Publishing with Kogan Page is very meaningful to me since they published Dr. Mee-Yan Cheung-Judge's *Organization Development: A Practitioner's Guide for OD and HR*, a work I referenced frequently early in my career. In this full circle moment, I am humbled to follow in her footsteps.

I'm also grateful for my teachers, Renoka Singh, Dr. John D. Carter, and Dr. William J. Rothwell, from whom I learned all things Organization Development, Applied Behavioral Science, and Gestalt OSD.

Special thanks to Aggie for the bakes and Aaron for the hugs. Above all, thank you, God. Couldn't say it any better than Psalm 113.

Introduction

Culture transformation is a journey that begins with a vision to change core experiences and processes in service to a business demand or directive. Businesses frequently modify their cultures to better engage their workforce, manage organizational issues, innovate, adapt to changes in the industry, and align with changing company strategy. Initiatives to reform an organization's culture successfully can boost employee morale, foster better teamwork and creativity, improve change adaptation, and, in the end, boost organizational performance and competitiveness; this can be achieved when taking an approach for transforming organizational culture through purpose, belonging, and impact.

Building a vibrant and inclusive culture is essential in today's dynamic organizational environment, and it has taken on great importance for leaders and practitioners alike. This book takes the reader on a tour of important topics that serve as the cornerstone of a comprehensive framework for changing organizational culture. Every subject is essential on its own, but is also entwined with organization development (OD) components to create a holistic strategy for cultural change using a framework with four interconnected pillars that may be used to shape cultural excellence and transformation anchored in empowered advocacy and socially meaningful projects. These pillars are:

1 Understanding psychological contracts;
2 Establishing psychological safety;

3 Cultivating cross-company partnerships;

4 Leveraging inclusive employee engagement.

A wide range of OD approaches are incorporated into this framework, including the use of the strengths of data-driven analysis, strategic interventions, and cooperative leadership. We'll walk through the challenges of change management, and the importance of encouraging candid dialogue and openness all along the way.

Employee enthusiasm and dedication are some of the many ingredients to help an organization grow; however, simply focusing on attracting and keeping talent is insufficient. The real difference between flourishing and merely going through the motions of the day-to-day lived experiences in organizations is in navigating a holistic, human-centered culture that encourages engagement, belonging, and a shared sense of purpose and that begins with building a foundational understanding of the power of psychological contracts and psychological safety.

Any healthy relationship must be built on the foundations of respect, trust, and fairness, and this is especially true in the workplace. This book explores the complexities of psychological contracts, which are unspoken agreements between workers and their employers, and how promoting psychological safety—an environment where people feel free to express their worries and take risks—is conducive to innovation and growth and serves as the cornerstone for genuine organizational transformation.

Once there is mutual trust, we can then focus on the role of employee engagement in socially impactful initiatives, which then allows us to explore methods for bringing corporate values and employee passions together that go beyond token volunteering. We can unleash the enormous potential of engaged employees as change agents by incorporating purpose into core business operations. We will examine the ways in which meaningful partnerships, real communication, and well-designed programs can foster this kind of involvement.

With an understanding of the drivers behind employee engagement, it is then possible to partner with employees differently, as catalysts for transformative and sustained change. Employees are strong change agents, not just parts of the corporate machine. We will discuss how to provide them with the knowledge and tools they need to support equity-based programs and promote inclusivity and diversity inside the company. One additional aspect of this is acknowledging and promoting the important function of employee resource groups (ERGs) as intermediaries for comprehending and magnifying the perspectives of the broader workforce, especially in diverse groups. Transforming an organization's culture is a team effort that frequently crosses organizational lines. We discuss how creating internal and external partnerships is essential to bringing about comprehensive change, emphasizing cooperation as the cornerstone of organization development by integrating partnership strategies based on OD methodologies.

As we work through these related subjects, we will uncover a holistic framework that recognizes the complexity of cultural transformation while also incorporating important organization development components, generating a strong and long-lasting strategy for positive change.

If you are a leader or changemaker, this book is an excellent manual and provides practical advice, examples from real-world situations, as well as the motivation to start your own cultural transformation journey. You can unleash the hidden potential in your organization and create a place where people thrive, communities flourish, and positive impact becomes the driving force behind success by embracing the interconnectedness of engagement, well-being, and advocacy.

Ready to change the culture in your organization? Well, let's get started.

1

A Holistic Framework for Transforming Organizational Culture

Culture change requires endurance, flexibility, and on occasion, a therapist. My tongue-in-cheek humor here is a serious nod to difficulties that may come up, depending on your race, gender, age, or other demographic as the one leading transformation initiatives. As a cisgender Afro-Caribbean female, I have had more than my fair share of turbulence engaging in this work and learned a lot about what it takes to be successful. That said, it might be hard to imagine a simple framework to navigate organization culture transformation, but when we distill down to the most important elements, they can be summarized in four high-level categories grounded in the principles of organization development (see Figure 1.1).

Understand Psychological Contracts

The first element in a holistic framework for transforming organizational culture is in understanding the role and influence of psychological contracts. Psychological contracts are the implicit expectations between employees and the organization (Rousseau, 1989). Developed by organizational psychologist Chris Argyris in the 1960s, the idea of a psychological contract is likely to be used around the workplace for a very long time. According to recent research on employee work engagement, employee engagement grows in environments where there are strong ties between an

FIGURE 1.1 A Holistic Framework for Transforming Organizational Culture

individual's values and those of the organization. When an employee chooses to work for a company and that organization chooses to hire them, there are unspoken, unwritten expectations on both sides that constitute the fundamentals of a psychological contract and can have a practical impact on the work experience.

Violations of psychological contracts have been linked to disruptive behaviors, lower job satisfaction, and higher intention to leave an organization. Companies may enhance employee retention and organizational performance by taking deliberate measures to comprehend employee expectations and manage them more effectively. Other than competitive pay, some areas to focus on are having a positive work environment, benefits for mental health and well-being, a sense of meaning and purpose in the day-to-day work, flexible work schedules, and more paid time off.

Engagement and Motivation

Studies conducted by Eisenberger et al. (2001) indicate that workers are more motivated, committed, and satisfied with their jobs when their psychological contracts are met. If these contracts are broken, there may be a decrease in engagement, withdrawal, and even increased turnover (Rousseau, 1995).

Productivity and Performance

A study conducted in 2002 by Conway and Briner discovered a positive relationship between worker productivity and the fairness of psychological contracts. Employees are therefore more likely to give their all and accomplish goals when they feel that their contributions are valued and that their expectations are met.

Organizational Health

According to Robinson (2004), a strong psychological contract is linked to a number of advantageous organizational outcomes, such as increased employee happiness, decreased conflict, and increased creativity. On the other hand, broken contracts may result in an unfavorable workplace atmosphere that raises stress levels, discourages teamwork, and eventually leads to an organization failing.

Employee Retention

As reported in research by Mathieu and Zajac (1990), a solid psychological contract plays a significant role in keeping employees on board. Employees are less inclined to look for work elsewhere when they feel appreciated, supported, and have the opportunity for advancement.

Recruitment and Employer Branding

Attracting top talent and enhancing employer branding can be achieved by cultivating a positive reputation for keeping psychological contracts. Organizations can attract and retain high-performing employees who make significant contributions to success by fostering a culture of trust and fairness.

When we consider culture transformation, diversity initiatives must be a part of the work. Broadly, the goal of diversity and inclusion (D&I) initiatives is to establish fair and inclusive work environments that support people from all backgrounds. Psychological contracts shape employee experiences and are an important but frequently ignored aspect in this journey. Recognizing and fostering these agreements can greatly improve the success of D&I projects.

Trust and Openness

Positive psychological contracts can translate into open channels for feedback and concerns and help in building trust in the leadership's dedication to equity in D&I contexts. Employee participation and engagement are more likely when they have faith in their company's commitment to hearing from and addressing their concerns.

Fairness and Equity

Having a contractual relationship with a specific set of terms may not be as important as knowing how employees perceive their shared responsibilities. A study by Robinson, Kraatz, and Rousseau (1994) indicates a significant relationship between managers' actions and employees' perceptions and fulfillment of their obligations by demonstrating how employer violations can affect employees' perceptions of their contracts. Therefore, the success of D&I initiatives depends on the perception of fairness in psychological contracts since feelings of exclusion can emerge from unmet expectations of fairness, which can impede the achievement of D&I objectives.

Feelings of Belonging and Shared Values

Psychological contracts can be strengthened with shared values and a sense of belonging, which could help employees extend their contributions when they feel acceptance and appreciation.

Communication and Transparency

Communication is crucial to preserving psychological contracts. This means being open and honest about the objectives of the organization, its progress, and the difficulties it faces in promoting inclusion. Employee engagement and trust are increased through open communication, which also helps them to understand their part in making the workplace more inclusive.

Accountability and Progress

To meet employee expectations, psychological contracts need accountability, and initiatives promoting diversity and inclusion need measurable outcomes. This reinforces the organization's dedication to inclusivity and shows that diversity and inclusion are real priorities, not just platitudes.

D&I initiatives can become embedded in the organization's culture and transcend from being programs by recognizing and fostering psychological contracts. Organizations can create a workplace that is more diverse, equitable, and successful by fostering trust, fairness, transparency, and accountability. This will allow each individual to feel valued, respected, and empowered to contribute.

Establish Psychological Safety

The next element in a holistic framework for transforming organizational culture is in establishing psychological safety. Creating an atmosphere where employees are free to express themselves, communicate ideas, and take chances without worrying about repercussions is at the heart of psychological safety (Edmondson, 1999). When it comes to fostering an atmosphere where people of marginalized identities can flourish, psychological safety has become somewhat more of a hot topic over time, particularly on social media. Feeling psychologically safe is simply knowing that one's words or actions are valid. No one should be punished for expressing their opinions or made fun of for having a unique perspective.

Businesses launch change projects for a variety of reasons, such as ensuring legal compliance, prevailing economic conditions, a desire for innovation, competing for market share, influencing social and community perception, and, of course, financial success. It is a good initiative in and of itself to give particular attention to psychological safety, but for it to be worth investing in, there needs to be a business case. As a result, studies have looked at the connection between psychological safety and outcomes like voice behaviors, staff attitudes, communication, creativity, and innovation (Newman, Donohue, and Eva, 2017).

Establishing a psychologically safe space necessitates paying careful attention to the complex experiences of all parties concerned, while also having an interest in changing those experiences extending beyond transactional exchanges toward more meaningful human connections; which is a shift in culture. Organizations seek longevity, resilience, and long-term viability in addition to profitability, and culture work can support these goals. Since initiatives to change culture are frequently met with opposition, doubt, and anxiety, focusing on psychological safety can be a key enabler for effective cultural transformation.

Accepting Innovation and Taking Chances

Changing a culture frequently means stepping outside of the comfort zone, accepting novel concepts, and taking measured risks. People who feel psychologically safe can express their worries, question presumptions, and try new things without being concerned about ridicule or holding others. This encourages an atmosphere of free inquiry and inventive problem-solving, which are essential for managing the different facets of change and is also a key ingredient for innovation.

Building Trust and Collaboration

Open communication and teamwork are encouraged when there is a culture of psychological safety that supports trust between individuals and groups. Building intergroup collaboration, dismantling organizational silos, and uniting disparate viewpoints around a common future vision all depend on this trust.

Improving Learning and Growth

Adapting to new working practices and learning new skills are frequently necessary as a result of change. Psychological safety establishes a secure environment where people may ask questions, get feedback, and make errors without worrying about facing consequences. This promotes a culture of ongoing learning, enabling people to successfully participate and adjust to an ever-changing environment.

Increasing Resilience and Adaptability

Shifting cultural norms can be an uncomfortable process leading to resistance and anxiety. People who are in psychological safety are better able to control their fears, recover from failures, and adjust to changing social standards. People with this resilience are better equipped to embrace change as an opportunity for personal development and improvement.

Recruiting and Retaining Talent

In the current competitive environment, talent gravitates toward companies that place a high importance on learning, cooperation, and open communication. These ideals are communicated via a culture of psychological safety, which draws and keeps top talent eager to adapt to a changing work environment and flourish there (Predictive Index, n.d.).

Psychological safety is not just a catchphrase but is essential and must be maintained for effective cultural transformation initiatives. Organizations can unleash the potential of their workforce, manage the challenges of change, and create a vibrant, flexible culture by making its development a top priority. Organizations that give thoughtful consideration to engaging in the cultivation and retention of psychological safety set themselves on a path to not just transform but also to unlock the excellence, creativity, and resilience that exist inside their people.

Cultivate Cross-Company Partnerships

The next element in a holistic framework for transforming organizational culture after taking deliberate steps to establish psychological safety is to cultivate cross-company partnerships. Organizational change is becoming a need rather than a luxury. In order to keep up with the constantly changing landscape of technology, market trends, and consumer expectations, businesses are looking more and more for partners to support their transformational projects. Of these, interorganizational collaborations have the most potential to spur creative thinking, quicken the pace of change, and ultimately lead businesses to long-term success. One way to introduce varied ideas into the company culture and to widen viewpoints is to promote cooperation and collaboration across organizations. Strong relationships between partners are essential for knowledge transfer to take place in coalitions (Inkpen and Dinur, 1998). Repeated transactions and previous partner interactions are factors that facilitate the formation of strong attachments (Gulati, 1995). Without strong links, partners may not form the relationships required for managers to voluntarily exchange knowledge, particularly in coalitions between rivals (Inkpen and Tsang, 2005). Strong links foster and improve reciprocity, trust, and long-term perspectives, as demonstrated by Larson (1992). A favorable correlation was observed by Kale, Singh, and Perlmutter (2000) between the degree of learning in coalitions and the strength of relationships.

General Stakeholder Identification

A comprehensive understanding of the stakeholders involved is crucial for the success of cross-company initiatives, which means identifying internal and external partners who can provide a range of viewpoints, knowledge, and resources to the change process. Asking questions about who will be affected by the project and its deliverables, how they will contribute to the success, and who should be given priority is a good place to start when identifying stakeholders. Identifying stakeholders is a deliberate and comprehensive process that goes beyond compiling a list; it takes into account inclusive methods of interacting with and utilizing knowledge. At a high level, consider the internal parties affected, including leaders who devise overall strategy, coordinate objectives, and promote internal collaboration. Employees are essential contributors to co-creation and implementation activities because they are close to the ground, so to speak. Functional teams such as marketing, IT, and HR are also essential.

Partnering with Employees

Broadly, partnerships begin with shifting your mindset around employees as simply workers to catalysts. In addition, without the support of workers throughout the organization, radical change attempts are likely to fail (Hill et al., 2012, p. 758). Gaining employees' commitment is particularly critical during radical change since it includes a fundamental, qualitative shift in the firm's philosophy or core perspective and strategic direction. Nonetheless, as radical organizational transformation is often launched by the top management team (TMT) and must subsequently be executed by workers at all levels of the company, there is a significant dynamic between the top management team and employees. According to research, workers' responses to change vary depending on to how far up the organizational ladder they are from the TMT. Intercompany collaborations provide a special chance to use the enormous potential embedded in the employee base. Through proactive engagement in the transformation process, companies may use their creativity, expertise, and dedication to initiate change from the ground up. Collaborative workshops, knowledge-sharing sessions, and exchange programs with partner organizations are effective ways to expand the skill sets and perspectives of employees. These kinds of activities are part of joint employee learning and development. Co-creation of transformation strategies, including staff members in the ideation and strategy development process, encourages ownership and buy-in, which results in change projects that are more successful and enduring.

Partnerships with Leaders at All Levels

Creating bridges with leaders at all levels in the organization can help to ensure that corporate goals and partnership objectives are aligned. Combined taskforces comprising specialized teams can promote cooperative problem-solving. It's essential to have an iterative approach that starts with a stakeholder assessment for the project in order to identify and confirm who should be participating based on level: executive leaders, senior leaders, middle managers, chiefs of staff, executive assistants, and individual contributors; business unit including the revenue engine, human resources, and social collectives; and, most importantly, the partnership needed with yourself.

Partnering with Employee Resource Groups

One opportunity that many organizations miss is the chance to partner with employee resource groups (ERGs). ERGs usually concentrate on the social employee experience aspects, aiming to foster a sense of community through networking events and forming relationships with others who have similar interests or backgrounds. ERGs gradually broaden their scope to incorporate member career development programs and a greater emphasis on outreach to external communities. Mature and forward thinking organizations have ERGs involved in projects meant to better connect corporate objectives and business priorities, often through ERG summits. The number of firms that now host an annual leadership conference for their ERG leaders has significantly increased since 2015. ERGs can help advance diversity and inclusion and business goals, resulting in a more creative and equitable workplace. Collaborating with ERGs on social impact projects or community development projects may improve a company's reputation while increasing employee engagement. Inclusive transformation can be enabled through employee groups' involvement throughout the course of a given change process. More specifically, ERG leadership summits are more than simply a chance for leaders to get together; they also serve as a potent catalyst for introducing them to prospects for strategic collaboration between other ERGs and the larger business. These summits often bring together the leaders of ERGs to hear from corporate executives, learn about diversity and inclusion goals, network with other ERG leaders, and host panels with ERG leaders at other businesses.

Cross-company partnerships are more than just tactical collaborations; they are strategic opportunities to spur innovation, uncover collective wisdom, and create long-lasting change. Actively involving stakeholders at all levels—from executives and staff to ERGs—allows businesses to forge solid alliances that enable them to unlock new opportunities, manage change's challenges, and emerge stronger and more resilient in a constantly changing business environment.

Leverage Employee Engagement for Sustained Implementation

The final element in a holistic framework for transforming organizational culture is to leverage employee engagement for sustained implementation. With OD approaches, change begins from the bottom up, purposefully soliciting input (insights and comments) from those who will ultimately carry out the improvements the company is trying to accomplish. This strategy was chosen, in part, because direct stakeholder participation increases the likelihood that the change will be accepted and maintained. There will always be some people who disagree with every change endeavor, but by being inclusive, you may significantly lower the "noise" and increase preparedness. According to Armenakis, Harris, and Mossholder (1993), being prepared for change can help reduce the possibility of opposition to it, which could lead to greater success in change initiatives. Knowing what captivates employees' attention and maintains their involvement is crucial when it comes to motivating them to take part in socially conscious projects. Many businesses invest time and resources in learning about the opinions of their employees year-round, and there is a selection of quarterly, bi-annual, yearly, and pulse surveys, which mostly ask about an employee's opinions about their supervisor, team, and culture. Certain polls also ask about sentiments related to inclusion and belonging. Nevertheless, I haven't seen many employee engagement surveys that ask about how satisfied employees are with the present social impact efforts, nor have I seen any businesses solicit employee interest in certain issues through crowdsourcing.

Understanding employee engagement is paramount for change initiatives. Research conducted by Kahn (1990) highlighted the concept of psychological availability, which is the physical, emotional, or psychological means to actively participate at a given time. It gauges an individual's level of engagement readiness in light of the distractions they encounter as part of social systems. People in this study were more or less able to immerse themselves completely in role-plays based on how they managed the different demands of their life, both at work and outside of it. As you embark on this transformation journey, keep in mind the psychological availability of yourself and those you will partner with.

When taken together, each part of the framework offered in this book will allow you to dive into what it takes for a successful culture transformation. The book concludes with a chapter that offers a fantastic case study of Fitbit's cultural revolution that mirrors the framework outlined. More specifically, it shows the most important components, actions, and attitudes required to lead you through the process in the fastest, most practical amount of time. The unique presentation of the content is captured in a podcast-style conversation between Marie Carasco, the author, and Jaison Williams, the

SVP of talent management, capabilities, and culture at Expedia Group. Before joining that executive team, Williams was the vice president of talent management and inclusion Fitbit, which is now a part of Google. If the same levels of diligence, partnership, and flexibility are applied to your organization transformation initiatives, nothing should hinder you from obtaining similar if not better results.

References

Armenakis, A. A., Harris, S. G., and Mossholder, K. W. (1993). Creating readiness for organizational change. *Human Relations*, **46** (6), 681–709.

Conway, N. and Briner, R. B. (2002). A meta-analysis of the relationship between psychological contracts and work outcomes. *Personnel Psychology*, **55** (1), 123–52.

Edmondson, A. (1999). Psychological safety and learning behavior in work teams. *Administrative Science Quarterly*, **44** (2), 350–83.

Eisenberger, R., Huntington, R., Hutchison, S., and Sowa, D. (2001). Perceived organizational support and psychological contracts: A theoretical integration. *Journal of Management*, **27** (6), 565–94.

Gulati, R. (1995). Does familiarity breed trust? The implications of repeated ties for contractual choice in alliances. *Academy of Management Journal*, **38**: 85–112.

Hill, N. S., Seo, M. G., Kang, J. H., and Taylor, M. S. (2012). Building employee commitment to change across organizational levels: The influence of hierarchical distance and direct managers' transformational leadership. *Organization Science*, **23** (3), 758–77.

Inkpen, A. C. and Dinur, A. (1998). Knowledge management processes and international joint ventures. *Organization Science*, **9**: 454–68.

Inkpen, A. C. and Tsang, E. W. (2005). Social capital, networks, and knowledge transfer. *Academy of Management Review*, **30** (1), 146–65.

Kahn, W. A. (1990). Psychological conditions of personal engagement and disengagement at work. *Academy of Management Journal*, **33** (4), 692–724.

Kale, P., Singh, H., and Perlmutter, H. (2000) Learning and protection of proprietary assets in strategic alliances: Building relational capital. *Strategic Management Journal*, **21**: 217–37.

Larson, A. (1992). Network dyads in entrepreneurial settings: A study of the governance of exchange relationships. *Administrative Science Quarterly*, 37: 76–104.

Mathieu, J. E. and Zajac, D. M. (1990). A review and meta-analysis of the antecedents, correlates, and consequences of organizational commitment. *Psychological Bulletin*, 108 (2), 171–94.

Newman, A., Donohue, R., and Eva, N. (2017). Psychological safety: A systematic review of the literature. *Human Resource Management Review*, 27, (3), 521–35, https://doi.org/10.1016/j.hrmr.2017.01.001 (archived at https://perma.cc/T3DU-SS5K)

Predictive Index. (n.d.) Psychological Safety, https://www.predictiveindex.com/blog/psychological-safety/ (archived at https://perma.cc/YH7J-7TWE)

Robinson, S. L. (2004). Trust and the psychological contract. *Journal of Organizational Behavior*, 25 (8), 939–56.

Robinson, S. L., Kraatz, M. S., and Rousseau, D. M. (1994). Changing obligations and the psychological contract: A longitudinal study. *Academy of Management Journal*, 37 (1), 137–52.

Rousseau, D. M. (1989). Psychological and implied contracts in organizations. *Employee Responsibilities and Rights Journal*, 2: 121–39.

Rousseau, D. M. (1995). *Psychological Contracts in Organizations: Understanding Written and Unwritten Agreements*. Sage Publications.

2

The Role of Employee Engagement in Socially Impactful Initiatives

The History of Corporate Social Responsibility

The idea of social equity has drawn a lot of attention lately, leading businesses to implement programs that advance justice, inclusivity, and equal opportunity. A key component of successfully implementing such strategies is staff involvement. This chapter seeks to emphasize the significance of employee engagement in promoting socially impactful initiatives, including aspects of corporate social responsibility and the influence of diversity and inclusion on organizational culture.

Since firms are being held more accountable for their impact on the environment and society, corporate social responsibility, or CSR, has been front and center. The idea of CSR dates back to the early 1900s, when a few progressive businessmen realized that companies had a responsibility to improve society. Robert Owen, a Welsh industrialist who supported social reforms and workers' rights during the Industrial Revolution, was one prominent player in this area. Social responsibility, according to Owen, placed a strong emphasis on treating employees fairly, on public health, and on education. In the early 1900s, the idea of corporate social responsibility started to take root in the United States. A number of prominent businessmen launched socially conscious projects in response to growing worries about worker exploitation and subpar working conditions. For example, in

1903, the National Cash Register Company, led by its founder John H. Patterson, pioneered programs including welfare facilities and employee profit sharing for workplace safety.

The corporate landscape would see enormous changes following World War II. During this time, the development of stakeholder theory was significant in influencing how CSR is understood today. In his groundbreaking book, *Social Responsibilities of the Businessman*, published in 1953, Howard R. Bowen made the case that companies ought to consider the interests of all parties involved, not just shareholders. This signaled a change in emphasis from maximizing profits to addressing more general socioeconomic issues.

CSR became popular in the latter half of the 20th century as a result of numerous environmental and social initiatives, and greater awareness of social justice was brought about by the environmental, feminist, and civil rights movements. Companies started to see the connection between their prosperity, the health of the environment, and society. As a result, many businesses began using CSR strategies such as ethical supply chain management, sustainable business practices, and philanthropy.

The development of CSR was further aided by the globalization process, which was marked by a rise in interconnection and international trade. Pressure on multinational firms to address social and environmental issues in their international operations was growing. The Global Compact, a voluntary program launched by the United Nations in 2000 to encourage firms to implement sustainable and socially responsible policies, further cemented the significance of CSR on an international level.

Throughout history, CSR has changed dramatically, moving from early attempts to enhance working conditions to the current emphasis on sustainability and stakeholder participation, and knowing the background of CSR helps us recognize the accomplishments as well as the obstacles still to be overcome. A dedication to CSR is still essential for building a more just and sustainable future as companies manage increasingly complicated societal and environmental concerns. Furthermore, the field of CSR is constantly changing, presenting both new possibilities and obstacles. The emphasis is now more on generating shared value, incorporating environmental and social objectives into fundamental business models, and assessing the results of CSR activities. Even if CSR has a complicated and varied past, it is evident that the idea has advanced significantly. From the earliest charitable endeavors to the current emphasis on generating shared wealth, companies are realizing more and more that they have an obligation to support a fair and sustainable future, which is at the root of social impact work.

Motivation and Engagement

Now, think about the last time you put your time and energy into something that was meaningful to you. What were the things that allowed you to stay focused with sustained interest? Was it something that tends to bring joy or fulfillment to you or someone else? Something that allows you to use specific skills? Or something that you want to see altered or changed? We humans tend to be motivated to engage in certain activities either intrinsically or extrinsically. The urge to accomplish something because it is inherently intriguing, fulfilling, or delightful as opposed to being driven by pressure or rewards from outside sources is known as intrinsic motivation. It's the reason you paint for hours on end even knowing you'll never win a skill-based painting competition, or why you hike a mountain just for the satisfaction of feeling the wind on your face, or the stones under your feet. Our innate curiosity, creativity, and enthusiasm are fed by this desire. "Intrinsic motivation is the motivation to do something for its own sake, for the sheer enjoyment of the task itself. Extrinsic motivation is the motivation to do something in order to attain some external goal or meet some externally imposed constraint" (Hennessey et al., 2015).

When it comes to employee motivation to participate in socially impactful initiatives, it's important to understand what drives their interest and sustains their engagement. The emotional attachment a worker has to their company, which leads to more voluntary effort and commitment, is known as employee engagement. Fostering a healthy business culture is essential for increasing employee engagement and for advancing efforts centered around social fairness.

Engaged workers are more inclined to support diversity, confront prejudices, and help foster an inclusive workplace. Engaged workers embrace fair procedures and policies that benefit all workers because they recognize and appreciate social equality. "Schaufeli et al. (2002) defined engagement as a positive, fulfilling, work-related state of mind that is characterized by vigor, dedication, and absorption" (Carasco-Saul, Kim, and Kim, 2015, p. 74). They continued by stating that having a lot of energy and mental fortitude when working, being eager to put effort into one's work, and persevering through challenges are characteristics of vigor. A feeling of importance, zeal, inspiration, pride, and challenge are traits of dedication. When we are completely focused and absorbed in a task, time flies by and we find it difficult to step away from it. This is known as absorption. Taking these factors into account, we can surmise that when an employee is motivated, and puts forth a fair amount of energy, persistence, and enthusiasm toward a cause that they have a hard time detaching from, then you've likely identified an area of significance and interest to them. In other words, without understanding the anchors of employee engagement in socially impactful initiatives, your company runs the risk of supporting initiatives that do not matter to your workforce.

Many companies put time and money toward understanding employee sentiments throughout the year. There are pulse surveys, quarterly, biannual, and even annual surveys to choose from. Most surveys cover how an employee feels about their team, boss, and culture. Some surveys also cover things like feelings around belonging and inclusion. However, I've not come across many employee engagement surveys that capture employees' satisfaction with the current social impact initiatives, nor have I seen companies crowdsource employee interest in specific causes. That said, one could argue that the annual fundraising and matching programs that many companies offer might be meeting that need. For example, "To support our employees' passion for giving, Microsoft matches employee donations of time and money to nonprofit organizations. Each October, our fun and spirited employee Giving Campaign—a tradition since 1983—makes a significant annual impact in addition to generous giving year-round" (Microsoft, 2023).

While these efforts certainly have merit, they are not the type of social impact initiatives I am referring to:

> [C]orporations commonly adopt social initiatives as a way to reduce pressures on the firm to be socially responsible. In addition, these actions not only serve to reduce immediate pressures placed on the firm, but, at the organizational field level, play a role in shaping what it means for a corporation to be socially responsible and thereby influences the intensity and nature of the pressures placed on firms. To the extent that these social initiatives are not "meaningful" in their potential for an efficient and effective positive impact on society, then corporations maintain or gain their legitimacy without providing a real benefit to society (Hess and Warren, 2008).

However, "although some firms will make sincere efforts to improve societal welfare, others may simply use social initiatives as symbolic devices that play a role in the larger debate over social responsibility" (Hess and Warren, 2008).

A major factor in the advancement of CSR programs is employee involvement. Employee engagement increases the likelihood that they will support the organization's objectives and values, particularly its dedication to social justice. Employees who connect with the company's CSR programs and feel a sense of purpose are great advocates for social equity both inside and beyond the business. Engaged employees further strengthen the organization's social equity–based initiatives by contributing to a positive social effect through volunteering, fundraising, and social cause advocacy.

Don't get it twisted; social impact as an area of focus is good for business, especially in the consulting world. In fact, firms like Boston Consulting Group (BCG) offer social impact services to help "clients transform their core business to create positive economic, environmental, and societal impact in ways that are profitable for the long term" (Boston Consulting Group, 2023). Their services focus on seven areas:

- **Food systems and security** includes sustainable agriculture, food loss and waste, food supply chains, and food packaging.

- **Humanitarian response** includes partnerships with NGOs and governments, experts in specific areas, and using the latest technology and data analytics.
- **Sustainable finance and investing** includes enterprise investment strategies.
- **Diversity, equity, and inclusion** includes supplier diversity, inclusive product design, gender equality, racial equality, and measurement of diversity and inclusion.
- **Global health** includes pandemic response, emergency prevention/preparedness, and humanitarian response.
- **Economic development** includes public-private partnerships, financial inclusion, and innovation in job creation and entrepreneurship.
- **Climate risk, adaptation, and resilience** includes assessing exposure to climate risks, developing responses, and mobilizing funding in order to build maximum protection for people, the economy, and natural ecosystems.

At the other end of the spectrum, we have an organization like Thomson Reuters that has a Social Impact Institute:

> Thomson Reuters is one of the only companies in the world that helps its customers pursue justice, truth, and transparency. [They] help uphold the rule of law, turn the wheels of commerce, catch bad actors, report the facts, and provide trusted, unbiased information to people all over the world (Thomson Reuters, 2023a).

Their approach (Thomson Reuters, 2023b) is rooted the UN's 17 Sustainable Development Goals, summarized by National Geographic (2023):

- **Goal 1: No Poverty.** End poverty in all its forms everywhere.
- **Goal 2: Zero Hunger.** End hunger, achieve food security and improved nutrition, and promote sustainable agriculture.
- **Goal 3: Good Health and Well-being:** Ensure healthy lives and promote well-being for all at all ages.

- **Goal 4: Quality Education.** Ensure inclusive and equitable quality education and promote lifelong learning opportunities for all.

- **Goal 5: Gender Equality.** Achieve gender equality and empower all women and girls.

- **Goal 6: Clean Water and Sanitation.** Ensure availability and sustainable management of water and sanitation for all.

- **Goal 7: Affordable and Clean Energy.** Ensure access to affordable, reliable, sustainable, and modern energy for all.

- **Goal 8: Decent Work and Economic Growth.** Promote sustained, inclusive, and sustainable economic growth, full and productive employment, and decent work for all.

- **Goal 9: Industry, Innovation, and Infrastructure.** Build resilient infrastructure, promote inclusive and sustainable industrialization, and foster innovation.

- **Goal 10: Reduced Inequality.** Reduce inequality within and among countries.

- **Goal 11: Sustainable Cities and Communities:** Make cities and human settlements inclusive, safe, resilient, and sustainable.

- **Goal 12: Responsible Consumption and Production.** Ensure sustainable consumption and production patterns.

- **Goal 13: Climate Action.** Take urgent action to combat climate change and its impacts.

- **Goal 14: Life Below Water.** Conserve and sustainably use the oceans, seas, and marine resources for sustainable development.

- **Goal 15: Life on Land.** Protect, restore, and promote sustainable use of terrestrial ecosystems, sustainably manage forests, combat desertification, and halt and reverse land degradation and biodiversity loss.

- **Goal 16: Peace, Justice, and Strong Institutions.** Promote peaceful and inclusive societies for sustainable development, provide access to justice for all, and build effective, accountable, and inclusive institutions at all levels.

- **Goal 17: Partnerships to Achieve the Goal.** Strengthen the means of implementation and revitalize the global partnership for sustainable development.

Company initiatives aimed at promoting diversity and inclusion are intimately related to employee engagement, as employee engagement increases the likelihood that they will accept and value diversity in the workplace. Actively seeking out different viewpoints, challenging prejudices, and fostering an inclusive workplace are characteristics of engaged employees. Because it gives all employees an equal chance regardless of their backgrounds, inclusion in turn promotes social fairness. Companies can access a diverse range of experiences and ideas by actively incorporating employees in diversity and inclusion programs. This will ultimately result in improved decision-making and a more equitable workplace.

Engaging Employees in Social Change Initiatives

The modern workforce is driven by a strong desire to have a purpose that goes beyond daily responsibilities. Millennials and Generation Z in particular are drawn to companies that share their values and have a positive social impact. This offers organizations a critical chance to harness the powerful energy of employee involvement in social change projects, and initiatives for social change are becoming more and more important to organizations. These programs support businesses' long-term viability and success in addition to having a positive social impact, and the active participation and engagement of employees is a critical component in their success. Within their organizations, employees have the ability to be agents of change; they are representatives of the company's mission and ideals, not just regular people carrying out their duties. Employees who actively engage in social change programs become agents of positive change, embodying the company's dedication to making a difference. Employees contribute to the company's social impact objectives when they participate in social change projects and use their special knowledge, abilities, and viewpoints to bring about significant change. Employees also take an active role in social responsibility initiatives, taking pleasure in a company's dedication to changing the world. Given all of this, how can we bring this potential to life and kindle a sense of dedication among our teams? In order for employees to participate in social change efforts, firms need to use a variety of approaches. At a high level, to start, gain an understanding of the inner and extrinsic variables that drive employee engagement as well as the personal values and organizational incentives that encourage employee participation. You'll then want to develop a strong social change plan by learning how to match your programs with the interests of your staff, and provide a variety of opportunities for participation, which will encourage a culture of purpose-driven action. Finally, you'll want to assess impact and recognize accomplishments along the way.

The Intrinsic Call: Values, Purpose, and Meaning Making

Employees are people looking for purpose and fulfillment, not merely parts in a money-making machine. Research on "prosocial motivation," such as that conducted by Grant (2008), shows how human beings naturally want to interact with others and make a difference in the world. This underlying incentive is a potent source of intrinsic motivation for employee engagement, and it fits in nicely with the quest of social change. Employee motivation increases when their personal values align with the organization's social change objectives. By connecting tasks to employees' sense of purpose and providing opportunities for significant contributions, organizations may capitalize on their intrinsic drive.

The Extrinsic Push: Incentives, Recognition, and Belonging

Enhancing employee engagement can be achieved by offering recognition, a sense of community, and extrinsic rewards. Acknowledging and recognizing staff members for their contributions to social change projects strengthens their dedication and promotes a culture of gratitude. Even though inner motivation is the foundation, extrinsic variables can be very important in igniting interest and maintaining momentum. Plausible incentives such as paid volunteer time, opportunities for skill development connected to social change projects, and public acknowledgment of staff contributions are great options. Providing these kinds of rewards fosters a sense of pride and community, which can increase participation.

Create a Compelling Social Change Strategy

Organizations need to be clear about their own commitment to social change before they can engage employees. Employee engagement is based on a clear and compelling social change approach and should be in line with the mission, values, and long-term objectives of the business. Organizations can encourage employees to actively participate and contribute by outlining the initiatives' goals and purpose in plain and concise terms. It's critical to articulate your goal clearly, make sure it fits with your fundamental beliefs, and communicate it well.

Employees are more inclined to stick with a company that supports causes close to their hearts that encourage engagement, while disengaged workers can cost US businesses as much as $550 billion annually. The Engagement Institute—which consists of The Conference Board, Sirota-Mercer, Deloitte, ROI, The Culture Works, and Consulting LLP—conducted comprehensive research that emphasizes the significance of engagement for the bottom line (Bolden-Barrett, 2017). It's interesting to note that most respondents in the study were able to explain their lack of engagement and list compelling missions as one of their expectations from leadership. Therefore, in order to encourage employee involvement in social change efforts, positive leadership is essential. Leaders send a strong message to staff when they actively participate in these programs and show their commitment to them. It fosters a supportive environment, motivates staff engagement, and offers a forum for cooperation and creativity.

Keep in mind that there is no one-size-fits-all approach to this. Most employees want freedom and adaptability, so provide a wide range of interaction opportunities to suit varying time, ability, and interest levels. This might involve internal advocacy efforts, skill-based pro bono work, fundraising campaigns, volunteer opportunities, and even involvement in the creation of new social change projects.

Time is valuable and scarce. Recognize this and provide low-barrier, flexible access points for involvement. Take into account remote volunteering choices, micro-volunteering opportunities with less time commitments, and even lunchtime learning sessions on social impact themes. Finally, integrate social change across your company's operations. Promote candid discussion of social concerns, honor staff members' accomplishments, and acknowledge them as important agents of change. Promoting this culture encourages continued participation and fosters a feeling of purpose. Employees must also think that what they do actually matters. It's critical to regularly monitor the effects of your programs and provide concrete outcomes. Providing regular updates on progress toward improvement can encourage and maintain employee engagement.

Consider Employee Insights

The level of granularity presented in the areas focused on in the previous section might create a kind of narrow template for organizations to consider supporting and investing in. To expand the options, while cultivating an engaged workforce, your organization should consider aligning choices of social impact initiatives with employee interests. If your organization has surveys around engagement, identifying employee interests in social impact could be as easy as adding a question to that existing survey. But let me warn you—if your company has a reputation for not sharing survey results and not taking action from the data gathered from employees, don't bother. You'll only damage trust and erode confidence. I'd also extend a word of caution for companies that usually take action but may not be quite ready to leverage feedback from employees in this area. However, if your company is willing to take on a reasonably timed journey toward modifying the portfolio of social impact options you can leverage the following ideas to gather feedback from employees:

1 Regularly conducting surveys among employees to collect insights on various facets of the workplace, such as satisfaction with their roles, communication effectiveness, and the overall organizational culture, aligns with principles of organizational development. These surveys are intentionally crafted to evaluate the overall well-being of the organization and pinpoint areas for enhancement.

2 Integrating systems for 360-degree feedback allows employees to receive evaluations from their peers, managers, and subordinates. This comprehensive approach provides a holistic view of individual performance and fosters an environment centered on ongoing improvement.

3 Facilitating sessions with focus groups provides an interactive and qualitative platform for employees to express their thoughts. This method encourages open discussions, unveiling perspectives that may not emerge through conventional feedback channels.

4 Cultivating a culture of regular check-ins and one-on-one meetings between employees and supervisors promotes consistent communication. This not only facilitates the exchange of feedback but also nurtures professional growth and relationship building.

5 Fostering an environment with open-door policies encourages employees to comfortably share their thoughts directly with leadership. This level of accessibility promotes transparency and trust within the organization.

6 Offering platforms, whether physical suggestion boxes or digital tools, for employees to submit anonymous feedback or suggestions contributes to a culture of open feedback. This approach allows individuals to share insights without concerns about potential repercussions.

7 Hosting regular employee forums or town hall meetings provides an opportunity for leadership to share updates, and for employees

to voice their opinions. This live interaction enhances engagement and showcases a commitment to listening to employee concerns.

8 Conducting thorough interviews with departing employees can unveil valuable insights into organizational strengths and weaknesses. Analyzing this feedback informs strategies for talent retention and development.

9 Facilitating programs for peer-to-peer feedback enables colleagues to acknowledge and provide constructive input to each other. This approach fosters a positive workplace culture and encourages collaboration.

10 Aligning feedback mechanisms with assessments of training and development needs allows organizations to customize professional development programs to address specific employee requirements.

11 Establishing advisory groups comprised of employees from diverse departments and roles provides a structured platform for ongoing dialogue and collaboration. These groups offer insights into organizational challenges and contribute to decision-making processes.

12 Implementing brief, regular pulse surveys enables organizations to capture real-time feedback on specific issues or initiatives. This agile approach facilitates quick adjustments and demonstrates responsiveness to employee concerns.

By integrating these feedback mechanisms based on organization development approaches, companies can nurture a workplace culture that prioritizes continuous improvement, open communication, and employee engagement. That said, I acknowledge that these decisions are often complicated and may require board-level approval. I also recognize that there are both social and political implications to taking a public position with a particular stance; that's what social impact is all about. Therefore, your company and leadership will need the stamina and fortitude to navigate what can be a tumultuous reaction to decisions to support controversial positions such as Black Lives Matter, LGBTQ+ rights, political contributions and affiliations, commitments to diversity and inclusion, reproductive rights, labor practices, ethical sourcing, product safety, crisis response, or cultural appropriation to name a few. It behooves organizations to anchor and align their decisions on which social impact initiatives to pursue, first in the business's principles and values, and second in the broader definition of what it means to be socially responsible. At the end of this chapter, I provide a list of organizations that are integrating what I've shared, as well as other focus areas not yet highlighted.

While there are numerous companies with impactful social initiatives, the list highlights organizations that not only make a difference but also offer promising career starting points for those eager to contribute to positive change. Employee morale and corporate culture are greatly impacted by participation in social change projects; employees feel more fulfilled and satisfied at work when they actively participate in projects that reflect their beliefs and sense of purpose. Higher levels of staff motivation, productivity, and loyalty follow from this.

Additionally, through encouraging a shared commitment to having a good influence, social change programs help to create organizational culture. Employee pride in the firm is increased when they see how committed the corporation is to social responsibility. Social effect strengthens a work culture that is motivated by purpose and becomes an essential component of the company's identity.

Fostering employee interest in equity-based initiatives is largely dependent on employee participation. Employee engagement in programs that advance equity and justice is higher when they have a sense of purpose and alignment with the organization's values. By involving workers in these programs, companies may benefit from their varied viewpoints and experiences, fostering a more welcoming and socially conscious work environment. Through the engagement of employees as change agents, representatives of the company's principles, and collaborators on social impact initiatives, establishments may fully use their labor force. Organizations may encourage employee involvement in social change efforts by focusing on both intrinsic and extrinsic incentives, implementing well-defined plans, and receiving support from the leadership.

Employers may encourage their staff to participate as partners in social change projects by giving them chances to contribute and improve the world. This may be accomplished in a number of ways, including by creating employee resource groups centered around social issues, arranging volunteer programs, and planning community outreach activities. Organizations that actively include employees in these programs empower their staff and show that they are committed to bringing about positive change in society. The benefits to community outreach, corporate culture, and staff morale are incalculable. For those organizations that haven't yet done so, it might be time to make employee participation in social change projects top priority. Employers who adopt this strategy may help to improve the world while giving their staff members a sense of fulfillment, purpose, and group influence.

In conclusion, for social equity–based programs to be implemented successfully in businesses, employee participation is a crucial component. Employees actively contribute to the creation of a more equitable workplace by promoting corporate social responsibility, supporting diversity and inclusion, and cultivating a positive organizational culture. Employers who place a high priority on employee engagement stand to gain from a diverse and inclusive workforce as well as greater customer satisfaction and company reputation. For this reason, it is crucial that businesses make investments in employee engagement in order to propel social equity–based projects and build a fairer future.

The Impact of the Covid-19 Pandemic

The Covid-19 pandemic worsened social inequalities that were already present. Numerous social equity projects were established to redress the inequities and build a fairer and more inclusive society as businesses and marketing techniques adjusted to the new normal, starting with government support programs. For those impacted by the epidemic, the US CARES Act enhanced unemployment compensation (Congressional Research Service, 2020). The goal of this program was to lessen the financial challenges experienced by people who lost their jobs as a result of Covid-19. Globally, governments have undertaken a range of measures to bolster small enterprises, including subsidies, loans, and payroll assistance programs (OECD, 2020). These actions were intended to stop job losses and company closures, particularly in towns that were already at risk.

Numerous companies and firms, including internet behemoths like Google and Amazon, made large donations to nonprofits and relief funds (Google.org, 2020; Amazon, n.d.), with the goal of giving the pandemic-affected populations immediate assistance. Companies have also put in place employee support initiatives, such as flexible work schedules and mental health resources (Moss, 2022). These programs were designed to protect workers' health and productivity in trying times. Globally, networks of mutual aid have developed, bringing together members of the community to offer assistance and resources to those in need (Warzel, 2020).

These networks attempted to build community resilience and solidarity by attending to the urgent needs of the disadvantaged populace. For example, to guarantee food security for vulnerable communities, local food distribution networks were built by community organizations and agricultural cooperatives in order to alleviate the pandemic's disruptive effects on the food supply chain (International Labour Organization, 2020).

Inequities around internet access became very prominent during the pandemic. To close the digital divide caused by work-from-home policies and remote learning, nonprofits and NGOs launched digital inclusion initiatives to give underprivileged areas access to technology and internet connectivity (Liu et al., 2021). Additionally, initiatives were started by groups like Human Rights Watch and Amnesty International to defend the rights and welfare of disadvantaged populations that were disproportionately impacted by the epidemic (Amnesty International, 2021). The goal of these programs was to guarantee social services and healthcare education to all people equally.

Numerous social equity projects have been launched to address the discrepancies that have been brought to light by the Covid-19 pandemic and other socioeconomic injustices. In order to promote social fairness since the pandemic's breakout, government support programs, corporate social responsibility initiatives, community-based efforts, and nonprofit activities have all been vital. To create a society that is more inclusive and egalitarian, these activities must be continuously evaluated and improved, regardless of if we experience another event the likes of Covid-19 or not.

Organizations Leveraging Social Impact Initiatives Across Industries

- **Adidas** is renowned for its commitment to corporate responsibility, focusing on three key pillars: community involvement, employee engagement, and corporate giving. An illustration of their community commitment is the BOKS by Reebok program, designed to provide fitness access to children aged 5 to 12. The impacts of this initiative, such as improved memory and physical fitness, have been independently evaluated. Adidas extends similar impactful programs globally, with initiatives such as the Pakistan Women's Empowerment Program and SOS Children's Village.

- **A-LIGN**, since 2013, has been partnering with clients to support local charities nationwide. Recognizing the integral role of giving back, A-LIGN annually donates to charities like Junior Achievement and ASPCA during the holiday season. Beyond holidays, the company encourages year-round community service by granting a day off each month for employees to engage in volunteer activities. A-LIGN's commitment goes beyond mere participation, fostering lasting relationships with local service organizations.

- **Ben & Jerry's**, since its inception, has championed grassroots initiatives for social justice, environmental protection, and sustainable food systems. Their initiatives, such as "Justice ReMix'd," focus on criminal justice reform, addressing racial disparities. Employees actively participate in the Ben & Jerry's Foundation, reviewing grants for grassroots organizations, showcasing a dedication to social causes.

- **Burlington Stores** collaborates with Delivering Good, a national nonprofit, for its Burlington Coat Drive during the holiday season. Customers, associates, and vendors donate new and gently worn coats, benefiting local communities. With over 2.3 million coats collected to date, Burlington Stores makes a significant impact on neighbors in need of warmth.

- **CBRE** is committed to developing healthy communities by addressing environmental, economic, social, and other impacts. Through initiatives like the Green Machine Campaign, CBRE plants trees, supports shelter programs, and aids in disaster relief. These programs showcase CBRE's comprehensive approach to creating positive societal changes.

- **Cox Enterprises** contributes to social impact by supporting start-ups addressing environmental and social challenges. The Cox Enterprises Social Impact Accelerator, powered by Techstars, guides mission-driven startups in their early stages. Additionally, Cox Enterprises has a long-standing sustainability program and has invested over $100 million in sustainability and conservation projects.

- **Disney**, through its Aspire initiative, sponsors the most comprehensive employer education program in the country since 2018. Covering 100 percent of tuition costs, Disney empowers its workforce to pursue education, offering support services such as onsite study halls and private career coaching. The initiative demonstrates Disney's commitment to building futures and uplifting communities through workforce development.

- **Esri**, as the leading mapping technology company, focuses on designing a smarter future. Supporting organizations in conservation, education, and humanitarian affairs, Esri's technology aids in solving global problems. Notably, during the Covid-19 pandemic, Esri provided free access to its software, training, and technical assistance, contributing to efforts like Johns Hopkins University's Covid-19 dashboard.

- **Flatiron Health,** an innovative healthcare tech company, organizes and standardizes unstructured cancer data to accelerate research. Launched in 2012, Flatiron Health collaborates with the FDA, NCI, and top oncology companies, showcasing its commitment to improving cancer care and treatment.

- **F5 Networks** prioritizes social impact by offering paid time off for volunteering, donation matching, and engagement in philanthropic campaigns. Collaborating with NASCOP, F5 Networks aids in controlling HIV/AIDS through tech solutions, exemplifying its commitment to meaningful social contributions.

- **GO Foundation** unlocks the potential of national service through high-dosage tutoring, mentorship, and enriching opportunities. The GO AmeriCorps Fellowship allows new grads to engage in a year of impactful service, creating a lasting impact within communities. GO Foundation supports fellows beyond their service year, ensuring a smooth transition to their next career move.

- **Google,** pledging $1 billion to nonprofits in five years and committing to 1 million hours of employee volunteering, demonstrates a strong commitment to social responsibility. Google's environmental and ethical initiatives, including achieving 100 percent renewable energy in 2017, showcase a holistic approach to making a positive impact.

- **Groupon** emphasizes community involvement, adapting to challenges like the pandemic by organizing a Virtual Volunteer Week. Employees engaged in remote volunteering, demonstrating Groupon's creative and adaptable approach to social impact.

- **Herman Miller,** in addition to giving employees election day off for a Day of Purpose, actively contributes to its community by mass-producing masks for local organizations. The company's commitment extends to sustainable goals, as seen in their partnership with Fashion Pact and the launch of the Sustainable Style initiative.

- **IKEA** focuses on improving children's lives through initiatives addressing child labor practices and supporting UNICEF since the 1990s. Their "Let's Play for Change" initiative aims to provide safe spaces for children to play, demonstrating a sustained commitment to social responsibility.

- **JLL,** in its Global Sustainability Report, outlines commitments to environmental sustainability and community support. Initiatives like zero carbon emissions for UK workplaces and partnerships with organizations like REP and WiAM showcase JLL's dedication to diverse social impact efforts.

- **Kohl's** Cares program, initiated in 2000, raises funds through special merchandise collections to benefit health initiatives nationwide. Partnering with various organizations, Kohl's Cares focuses on educating children and families about wellness, childhood obesity, and chronic disease management.

- **LEGO,** committed to sustainability, partners with the World Wildlife Fund and uses sugarcane-based materials for its products. Pledging $15 million over 15 years to reduce its carbon footprint, LEGO exemplifies a toy company striving for a more sustainable future.

- **LinkedIn** achieves social initiatives through nonprofit partnerships and eco-friendly practices. With ambitious zero-waste goals and 80 percent renewable energy usage, LinkedIn integrates sustainability into its corporate culture.

- **NCR,** as a leading enterprise technology provider, established the NCR Foundation in 1953. The foundation grants support to nonprofit partners aligned with NCR's values, ensuring a commitment to innovation and community self-sufficiency.

- **The New York Times Neediest Cases Fund,** for over 100 years, has distributed generous donations from readers to global organizations providing direct assistance to those in need. The fund, supporting nonprofit organizations through campaigns and special grants, exemplifies the *New York Times'* commitment to social impact.

- **Nordstrom,** beyond its retail operations, actively contributes to communities. With increased clothing donations, volunteer hours, and ambitious sustainability goals, Nordstrom showcases a multi-faceted approach to social responsibility.

- **NRG,** as an energy provider, is dedicated to becoming a sustainable source of power. With clear goals like achieving net-zero emissions by 2050, NRG emphasizes the urgency of addressing climate change and documents its initiatives and results in annual sustainability reports.

- **Panasonic,** beyond its electronics brand, is committed to social impact through the Office of Social Impact. Initiatives like investing in Camp Skyhook and supporting the Students 2 Science Newark Technology Center showcase Panasonic's dedication to STEM education and community development.

- **Patagonia,** known for its sustainable practices, donates at least 1 percent of its sales or 10 percent of pretax profits to environmental grassroots groups. The company's commitment to social and environmental initiatives sets a standard in corporate responsibility.

- **PetSmart,** beyond being a pet store, supports animal-assisted therapy programs and provides access to assistance dogs for veterans. PetSmart Paws for Hope and partnerships like Canine Companions for Independence demonstrate the positive impact on lives through the power of animals.

- **Salesforce,** through its Philanthropy Cloud, donates over $250 million annually toward grants and education initiatives. The platform enables companies to organize social responsibility projects.

- **Schwan's Company,** recognized for products like Mrs. Smith's pies and Tony's pizza, through the Schwan's Corporate Giving Foundation actively contributes to local communities by directly supporting causes related to hunger alleviation and youth development. Over the last five years, Schwan's Food Company has generously donated more than 6 million pounds of food to Feeding America, in addition to supporting the School Nutrition Foundation through scholarships of up to $2,500 each. The company's dedication extends beyond its products in the freezer aisle, aiming to make a positive impact on lives.

- **Signify**, a leading force in lighting technology, champions social responsibility through the Signify Foundation. This nonprofit organization is committed to providing safe and sustainable lighting to underserved communities globally. The foundation goes beyond merely supplying lighting by offering essential, long-term, and affordable lighting solutions to areas facing adversity, including natural disaster zones. Moreover, the Signify Foundation plays a crucial role in training entrepreneurs in these regions, ensuring the sustainability and maintenance of the provided lighting.

- **Southwire** is dedicated to achieving the highest standards of excellence for its workforce by prioritizing environmental stewardship and corporate sustainability. The company's commitment to sustainability spans five key areas: Growing Green, Living Well, Doing Right, Giving Back, and Building Worth. Through a comprehensive approach, Southwire actively works to reduce its carbon footprint, foster a safe and inclusive workplace, maintain organizational transparency, engage staff in meaningful community service initiatives, and deliver top-quality service to customers and stakeholders.

- **Success Academy** stands as a beacon in public education, redefining possibilities and championing educational equity. As a leading public charter school system, Success Academy believes in the inherent potential of every child to learn and excel. Currently the fifth-largest public school system in New York State and consistently the highest performing, Success Academy ensures that every high school graduate attains college admission. Leveraging advancements in technology, business, and management, the academy remains committed to empowering children and offers diverse career opportunities in classrooms, schools, and the central office, where individuals can contribute significantly to social impact.

- **Synovus**, a regional financial services company serving communities across Georgia, Alabama, South Carolina, Florida, and

Tennessee, goes beyond banking to make a positive impact through its locally focused community outreach program, Here Matters. This program directs Synovus's volunteer and financial support toward three key areas: education, needs-based opportunities, and health and wellness. From supplying local food banks and schools with essential resources to providing financial literacy classes and college scholarships, Synovus is deeply committed to enriching and strengthening the numerous communities it serves.

• **Warby Parker**, renowned for its eyewear, goes beyond its "buy one, give one" initiative by actively engaging in a more comprehensive social mission. Through strategic programs and partnerships, the company trains individuals in over 50 countries to conduct eye exams and subsequently sells glasses at an affordable price. This approach empowers communities by creating sustainable income sources and ensuring broader access to eyewear. Having distributed over five million pairs of glasses since initiating this effort, Warby Parker's commitment to social impact is a major draw for individuals seeking meaningful work experiences.

References

Amazon (n.d.). 5 ways Amazon is helping to address U.S. communities' biggest challenges right now, www.aboutamazon.com/impact/community (archived at https://perma.cc/F5CL-HGCW)

Amnesty International (2021). Amnesty International Report 2020/21: The state of the world's human rights, www.amnesty.org/en/documents/pol10/3202/2021/en/ (archived at https://perma.cc/BC46-XKKQ)

Bolden-Barrett, V. (2017). Study: Disengaged employees can cost companies up to $550B a year. HR Dive, www.hrdive.com/news/study-disengaged-employees-can-cost-companies-up-to-550b-a-year/437606/ (archived at https://perma.cc/EK99-A7YV)

Boston Consulting Group (2023). Social Impact, www.bcg.com/capabilities/social-impact/overview (archived at https://perma.cc/4DAD-FVFA)

Bowen, H. R. (1953). *Social Responsibilities of the Businessman*. Harper.

Carasco-Saul, M., Kim, W., and Kim, T. (2015). Leadership and employee engagement: Proposing research agendas through a review of literature. *Human Resource Development Review*, **14** (1), 38–63.

Congressional Research Service (2020). Unemployment Insurance Provisions in the CARES Act, https://crsreports.congress.gov/product/pdf/IF/IF11475 (archived at https://perma.cc/8SD6-MTYT)

Google.org (2020). Our $100 million contribution to COVID-19 relief, https://medium.com/google-org/our-100-million-contribution-to-covid-19-relief-dea485a199d3 (archived at https://perma.cc/T44N-NF7D)

Grant, A. M. (2008). Does intrinsic motivation fuel the prosocial fire? Motivational synergy in predicting persistence, performance, and productivity. *Journal of Applied Psychology*, **93** (1), 48.

Hennessey, B., Moran, S., Altringer, B., and Amabile, T. M. (2015). Extrinsic and intrinsic motivation. *Wiley Encyclopedia of Management*. John Wiley and Sons, 1–4.

Hess, D. and Warren, D. E. (2008). The meaning and meaningfulness of corporate social initiatives. *Business and Society Review*, **113** (2), 163–97, https://onlinelibrary.wiley.com/doi/10.1111/j.1467-8594.2008.00317.x (archived at https://perma.cc/L2WK-499D)

International Labour Organization (2020). COVID-19 and the impact on agriculture and food security, www.ilo.org/wcmsp5/groups/public/---ed_dialogue/---sector/documents/briefingnote/wcms_742023.pdf (archived at https://perma.cc/6YB5-AAYE)

Microsoft (2023). The driving force behind our mission, www.microsoft.com/en-us/corporate-responsibility/philanthropies/employee-engagement (archived at https://perma.cc/5PJU-TNUU)

Moss, J. (2022). The pandemic changed us. Now companies have to change too. *Harvard Business Review*, https://hbr.org/2022/07/the-pandemic-changed-us-now-companies-have-to-change-too (archived at https://perma.cc/Y3WX-WSK9)

National Geographic (2023). Sustainable Development Goals, https://education.nationalgeographic.org/resource/sustainable-development-goals/ (archived at https://perma.cc/BHB8-XH7B)

OECD (2020). Turning hope into reality, www.oecd.org/economic-outlook/december-2020/ (archived at https://perma.cc/VU32-ADZ9)

Thomson Reuters (2023a). Social Impact Institute, www.thomsonreuters.com/en/about-us/social-impact.html (archived at https://perma.cc/4XVF-2548)

Thomson Reuters (2023b). Sustainable development at Thomson Reuters, www.thomsonreuters.com/content/dam/ewp-m/documents/thomsonreuters/en/pdf/corporate-responsibility/tr-social-impact-products-sdg-alignment-spring-2019.pdf (archived at https://perma.cc/3M74-ZQLS)

Warzel, C. (2020). Feeling powerless about Coronavirus? Join a mutual-aid network. *New York Times*, www.nytimes.com/2020/03/23/opinion/coronavirus-aid-group.html (archived at https://perma.cc/HU2T-TEPP)

3

Employees as Advocates of Equity-based Initiatives

If you're reading this book, it's likely that you're interested in taking an inclusive approach to your organization's change initiatives—a fantastic start to what could be a meaningful experience for you, and everyone involved. In the field of organization development (OD) culture transformation is at the heart of work and operationalized using inclusive practices to engage multiple stakeholders. OD takes a bottom-up approach to navigating change and deliberately asks for participation (insights and feedback) from the people who would ultimately implement the changes that the business is aiming to achieve. One reason for this approach is that when stakeholders have direct involvement, they are more likely to embrace and sustain the change. In any change initiative you'll have your fair share of nay-sayers; however, taking an inclusive approach can greatly reduce the "noise" and improve readiness. "[R]eadiness for change may act to preempt the likelihood of resistance to change, increasing the potential for change efforts to be more effective (Armenakis, Harris, and Mossholder, 1993).

Defining Diversity, Equity, Inclusion, and Belonging

DEIB, which stands for diversity, equity, inclusion, and belonging, is a comprehensive paradigm that tackles the many complexities of corporate culture. Diversity is the acknowledgment and appreciation of individual differences, including those related to race, ethnicity, gender, age, sexual orientation, and other factors (Cox and Blake, 1991). In order to achieve equity, one must guarantee just treatment, offer equal chances, and remove structural obstacles that support inequality (Bell, 1980). By establishing a setting where each person feels heard, respected, and appreciated, inclusion aims to promote a sense of belonging (Catalyst, 2021). In this sense, belonging goes beyond inclusion and emphasizes a strong bond and sense of acceptability among the group of employees (Thomas and Ely, 1996).

The Importance of DEIB Initiatives in Organizations

It is essential to put DEIB ideas into practice in order to promote an inclusive and respectful work environment. Diversity fosters creativity and problem-solving by bringing a variety of viewpoints, experiences, and ideas to the table (Kearney, Gebert, and Voelpel, 2009). Businesses that have diverse teams are more flexible, more equipped to handle difficult problems, and have an advantage over rivals in the global economy. By guaranteeing that every worker has an equal chance at development and promotion, equity helps to reduce differences that might result from institutional biases (Blau and Kahn, 2017). A dedication to fairness creates a meritocratic atmosphere in which ability and contributions are the main factors determining success, which boosts employee happiness and organizational commitment.

When inclusion is present, people feel more respected, welcomed, and free to be who they truly are at work (Catalyst, 2021). This fosters a sense of belonging. According to Mor Barak, Cherin, and Berkman (1998), inclusive workplaces have increased employee involvement, improved morale, and boosted cooperation. As a result, this enhances output and innovation, adding to the organization's success.

The Role of Employees as DEIB Advocates

Championing DEIB projects throughout their workplaces is a critical role played by employees, and increasing our colleagues' awareness and understanding is the first step toward advocacy. Workers have the opportunity to actively participate in discussions on the advantages of diversity, by exchanging personal stories, and encouraging an environment of transparency (Gardenswartz and Rowe, 1994). Employees may also help normalize inclusive practices and dispel preconceptions by serving as diversity ambassadors.

Additionally, staff members can assist in the creation and execution of diversity initiatives. According to Kulik, Roberson, and Perry (2007), this includes taking part in training sessions, offering input on projects, and actively helping to create a workplace that is more inclusive. Employees who serve as champions increase the impact of DEIB initiatives, sending ripples across the whole company.

The success of any company depends on embracing diversity, equity, inclusion, and belonging. These programs foster creativity, establish just and empowered work cultures, and improve the general well-being of employees. As advocates, workers are essential in creating and maintaining a culture that celebrates diversity and gives everyone a sense of inclusion. The joint efforts of the workforce and leadership are essential to accomplishing significant and long-lasting organizational change.

The Impact of DEIB Initiatives on Organizational Success

The chapter delves into the many advantages that come with implementing DEIB programs in enterprises. We can observe the critical function DEIB plays in promoting organizational success through an examination of financial results, creativity, problem-solving, employee engagement, and retention.

Understanding the Benefits of DEIB Initiatives

FINANCIAL BENEFITS

Through extensive research, McKinsey & Company (2020) found a link between financial success and leadership diversity. According to the survey, which included more than 1,000 large organizations in 15 countries, businesses with diverse leadership teams had a higher chance of outperforming their competitors in terms of profitability. These diversity leaders have one thing in common: they take calculated risks and have a methodical strategy to bolster inclusion. The paper identifies five areas of action based on these firms' best practices, which I support:

1 Make certain that a variety of talent is represented. This remains a crucial factor in promoting inclusivity. Diverse talent should be encouraged by companies to advance into executive, managerial, technical, and board positions. They should make sure that a strong I&D (inclusion and diversity) business case created for each company is approved and carefully consider which multivariate diversity dimensions should be given priority (e.g., beyond gender and race). They also need to set the right data-driven targets for the representation of diverse talent.

2 Boost the Inclusion and Diversity leadership's responsibility and skills. Outside the HR department or employee resource group leaders and companies should center their I&D efforts on their main business executives and managers. Furthermore, they want to bolster the inclusive leadership competencies of their executives and managers while also adamantly holding all leaders accountable for advancements in innovation and development.

3 Promote fairness and openness to allow for equality of opportunity. Companies must provide equal opportunities for promotion in order to move closer to a real meritocracy. They should use analytics tools to demonstrate the transparency and fairness of the procedures related to salary, promotions, and criteria; they should

also debias these processes and work toward achieving the diversity goals outlined in their long-term workforce strategies.

4 Encourage transparency and address microaggressions. In addition to actively assisting managers and employees in recognizing and resolving microaggressions, businesses should have a zero-tolerance policy for discriminatory behavior, including bullying and harassment. In addition, they ought to set expectations for cordial, open conduct and request that managers and staff rate one another's adherence to these standards.

5 Encourage a sense of belonging by firmly endorsing diversity. Businesses ought to foster an environment where workers feel free to be who they really are at work. In order to promote a feeling of community and belonging, managers should openly embrace and convey their dedication to various types of diversity. They should also establish connections with a diverse range of individuals and assist employee resource groups. Businesses should clearly evaluate belonging in polls conducted internally.

By offering insights into how diverse teams generate innovation and adaptation, which may eventually influence the bottom line, Shore et al. (2011) add to our knowledge of the impact of diversity on financial performance.

INNOVATION AND PROBLEM-SOLVING

According to a study by Thomas and Ely (1996), there are eight prerequisites that put organizations in a position to use identity group differences for organizational renewal and growth. These items are either the focus of leadership, the company culture, or the organization at large:

1 The leadership must recognize that a diverse workforce will represent a range of viewpoints and methods for doing tasks, and they must really cherish the diversity of ideas and insights.

2 The leadership must understand the opportunity for learning as well as the difficulties that an organization may face when various viewpoints are expressed.

3 Everyone must be expected to perform to high standards as part of the company culture.

4 The culture of the company ought to encourage personal growth.

5 Transparency must be promoted by the corporate culture.

6 The work environment ought to instill a sense of worth in employees.

7 The company must have a clearly defined mission that is shared by everybody.

8 The structure of the organization must be comparatively egalitarian and non-bureaucratic.

In the years since this work, so much has remained true and unrealized by companies that have not articulated or integrated a vision and purpose for a diverse workforce.

When it comes to problem-solving, I have a bit of a different side to highlight, and that thought is that without the support of those in the dominant ethnic representation, diversity work goes nowhere. In other words, the first problem to solve is in getting non-minority groups onboard. Plaut et al. (2011) provided evidence of both implicit and explicit links between multiculturalism and exclusion, as well as a relationship between perceived exclusion and responses to diversity; they conducted five studies that examined how White Americans, who belong to the dominant group, respond to diversity in comparison to the reactions of racial minorities. Their studies examined how White people's responses to diversity play a crucial role in the success or failure of diversity programs.

According to the U.S. Equal Employment Opportunity Commission (2007), about two-thirds of US workers in the private sector are White, and they are highly represented in professional positions (76 percent), mid-level management (81 percent), and executive and senior management (87 percent). This suggests that they control a significant portion of the power in US workplaces collectively. Organizations and educational environments cannot successfully negotiate and manage the complexity of diverse workforces and constituents without the cooperation of White people. Given the previously noted predicted enormous expansion in population diversity, failure of this kind might have dire political, social, and economic ramifications. Therefore, the true challenge in promoting diversity and inclusion is to comprehend how people respond to difference in order to develop diversity-related practices, policies, and messaging without alienating either group—a tall order indeed.

EMPLOYEE ENGAGEMENT AND RETENTION

Chapter 2 focused on the role of employee engagement in socially impactful initiatives. What I'd like to highlight here is employee engagement regarding DEIB efforts, specifically as it relates to the disconnect between HR leader perceptions on how well their organizations are doing with DEIB efforts vs. employee sentiment. Results from Gallup (2023) Research indicate that only 31 percent of workers believe their company is dedicated to enhancing racial justice or equality in the workplace, despite 84 percent of CHROs reporting that their companies are increasing investment in DEIB, which begs the question of employee expectations in this area. It starts with discrimination. The Gallup study highlights that discrimination at work is still a problem for both employees and HR directors; just 5 percent of HR leaders report having dealt with it in the previous year, compared to 16 percent of employees.

Another challenge is respect. Even if they think HR officials appreciate them, only 44 percent of employees feel respected, and 90 percent of those who don't feel respected report encountering discrimination at work, even though 60 percent of HR officials claim that employees are respected (Gallup, 2023). There is also a challenge with having DEIB conversations. I for one can attest to this, having had a senior leader express the sentiment of being offended when I asked his leadership team why DEIB was important to the company. Leaders and staff both want their managers to feel at ease when talking about DEIB, but while 41 percent of managers claimed to be prepared, just 39 percent of employees said their boss had discussed DEIB subjects with them in the previous year. Additionally, just 8 percent of HR directors said their managers felt ready. According to Gallup statistics, managers who have participated in a listening session, town hall, or company-wide meeting during the last year are more likely to be ready for DEIB talks. To address these challenges, metrics such as employee engagement surveys or inclusion indexes may be used to find perception gaps and help increase employee sentiment within the business. Compare these to rivals and assess against outside standards. Provide managers with additional training on inclusiveness, focusing on how to build local respect and trust with their teams. Pay attention to the special talents of every worker and offer appropriate training. By investing in tried-and-true manager development, you can equip managers with the knowledge and abilities needed to succeed by teaching them to engage in DEIB discussions. Don't let them feel inadequate to lead their teams; instead, try to instill confidence in them.

When we think about what it takes to retain ethnically diverse talent, it is important and reasonable to listen to, take seriously, and address their concerns. Your organization will also want to evaluate the lived experiences of underrepresented talent to improve in the areas of inclusion and belonging. I've attended what are sometimes called "roundtables," which are preplanned facilitated conversations between leaders in an organization and a specific ethnically diverse community. This approach can help in building trust through a meaningful two-way connection that allows leaders and employees to have a dialogue. However, exercise caution with this approach, since like any other employee listening system, you should be prepared to act on the things that can and should be addressed.

A number of other approaches with retention are anchored in financial incentives, but it is my humble opinion that no amount of compensation can make up for an unreasonably challenging work environment, although that will depend on one's values. That said, there are sentiments around the impact of mentoring and sponsorship programs in retaining diverse talent. I have mixed feelings about this. If the culture is plagued with systemic issues, mentoring might only provide some temporary coping strategies, and sponsorship may help with advancement into spaces where ethnically diverse talent is not welcomed and won't thrive.

Some of the systemic issues might be anchored in the ways White supremist culture shows up in organizations, which I discuss in Chapter 8, Elevating the Significance of ERGs. In my opinion, and based on the work of Okun (2001) the most problematic of the 15 characteristics of White supremacy culture that show up in organizations are:

- *Defensiveness*: criticizing persons in positions of authority is seen as offensive and threatening.

- *Only one right way*: the conviction that there is just one proper way to do things and that once people are shown it, they will realize it and follow it.

- *Paternalism*: those in positions of authority believe they are qualified to decide what is best for those who lack it, and people without power have little idea how those decisions are made or who makes them, but know how the decisions impact them.

- *Power hoarding*: the belief that there is little value in sharing power and when someone recommends making changes to the way things should be done in the company, individuals in positions of authority feel threatened because they believe it will reflect poorly on their leadership.

- *The right to comfort*: the belief that those with power have a right to emotional and psychological comfort, scapegoating those who cause discomfort.

When these particular elements show up in the culture, ways of working, and implicit expectations on how people of color are treated, it does no less than discourage advancement with DEIB initiatives, and essentially forces out anyone who would have the gumption to challenge the status quo.

The Role of Employees in DEIB Advocacy

There are several types of employee advocates in organizations, starting with internal advocates, defined broadly as individuals who actively support and promote the goals, values, and activities of the company. They can be very helpful in creating a positive culture when they interact with coworkers and could assist in coordinating team efforts with corporate goals.

Employee advocates can be motivated by a whole host of things, including values, sense of belonging, and career advancement.

Brand advocates are workers who promote and represent the company outside of their workplace. They often tend to engage in marketing initiatives, share positive experiences, and contribute to improving the company's standing with clients and the general public.

Diversity and inclusion advocates are employees devoted to promoting an inclusive and diverse workplace by actively encouraging and supporting programs that advance inclusion, equity, and diversity. They may also call out inequities to bring light to the challenges faced by marginalized groups in the company.

Innovation advocates are workers who support innovation, creativity, and ongoing development within the company and are concerned about seeing ongoing organizational progress.

Wellness advocates are staff members committed to enhancing mental and physical health at work. They promote work-life balance, endorse health and wellness initiatives, and help create a welcoming environment where the welfare of employees is given first priority.

Sustainability advocates are workers who actively support and participate in environmentally friendly measures inside the company. They encourage eco-friendly practices, back environmental responsibility, and promote the organization's dedication to social and environmental sustainability.

These are just some of the types of employee advocates that exist in organizations, all of whom are essential to the success and reputation of an organization, as well as the corporate culture and the reinforcement of values. You'll want to consider which employee advocate types would be helpful partners for your culture transformation initiatives.

CASE STUDIES

The Reboot Representation Tech Coalition

There are a number of organizations that can serve as exemplars of how to engage employees in advocacy, as well as a number of initiatives from which to glean insights on what is possible. One such initiative is the Reboot Representation Tech Coalition, which is a partnership of leading tech companies that have joined together to combat the gender gap for underrepresented women of color in technology by maximizing their effect, coordinating their objectives, and pooling their resources. The Coalition's first significant project is a three-year initiative to double the proportion of Black, Native American, and Latina women in the United States obtaining bachelor's degrees in computers by 2025. Without this initiative, the proportion of underrepresented women of color earning degrees in computing would not double until 2052, which would have a significant financial impact on both the industry and society.

IBM

Global technology and consulting firm IBM approaches DEIB holistically, emphasizing inclusive leadership, supplier diversity, and equitable opportunities. One of their projects is their Call for Code Racial Justice program, a global endeavor that invites developers and entrepreneurs to propose solutions addressing racial inequity and supporting justice. The goal of this project is to utilize technology to fight systematic racism and promote significant change. It is urged of participants to create apps and solutions addressing problems including equitable access to opportunity, criminal justice reform, and police accountability. IBM offers assistance, materials, and knowledge to help transform these concepts into practical, effective ways to advance racial justice (IBM, 2020).

IBM Employee Advocacy Involvement

IBM has a focus on both representation and retention through development by way of sponsorships and mentorships. This involves intentionally focusing on their employee professional advancement.

Procter & Gamble (P&G)

P&G, a consumer goods company, is demonstrating their commitment to diversity and inclusion with a number of resources that include access to "Courageous Conversations," an online training initiative focused on racial bias education, aiming to create a more inclusive workplace and impact communities of color (Procter & Gamble, 2023a). In order to promote knowledge and understanding, staff members actively participate in training programs, have candid conversations about racial issues, and support outreach projects in the community. Successes include improved cultural competency among employees and increased support for minority-owned businesses. P&G has pledged to raise its yearly spending with diverse-owned companies to $5 billion by 2030 (Procter & Gamble, 2023b). Challenges for companies like P&G involve addressing deep-seated biases and ensuring sustained commitment.

Bank of America

Bank of America, a global financial institution, launched the "Racial Equality and Economic Opportunity Initiative" in June 2020. Through a company-wide commitment to promote racial equality and economic opportunity across various communities, Bank of America is dedicated to tackling the underlying causes of inequality. This initiative focuses on investing in minority communities, supporting affordable housing, and addressing economic disparities. Employees support equitable employment practices, volunteer for community development initiatives, and take part in mentoring programs. They also run financial literacy initiatives for marginalized groups (Bank of America, 2023). Successes include investments financing bonds and equity funds with an emphasis on environmental and racial fairness; collaborations assisting businesses, schools, and universities that prioritize employer upskilling and skill development for a diverse student body such as indigenous students in the Navajo nation through New Mexico University; and awards enabling people and neighborhood groups to expand their goals and influence. Challenges involve navigating complex socioeconomic issues and ensuring long-term sustainability.

Target Corporation

Target, a retail company, has a comprehensive DEIB strategy, with a significant focus on the Black community. Their initiatives, such as "Racial Equity Action and Change," have several focus areas including the Target Scholars initiative introduced in April 2021 in collaboration with the United Negro College Fund (UNCF) to provide scholarships to students attending historically black colleges and universities. They enlarged the program in May 2022 to give the almost 1,000 scholars greater assistance and extensions, and also introduced a new Target Scholars Sophomore Internship program in November 2022 (Target, 2023). Staff members take an active involvement in community outreach, internal mentorship programs, and diversity councils.

"When individuals feel the need to suppress their true selves, the lack of authenticity can also spread to other parts of the workplace, putting an emotional toll on individuals that can lead to reduced morale, increased stress, and negatively impact their overall mental well-being." (Gonzales, 2023). This is the result of covering. In order to fit in with the dominant or majority group, covering refers to downplaying or reducing one's apparent or unseen different qualities. This frequently happens when members of marginalized groups hide facets of who they are—race, gender, sexual orientation, or disability—in an effort to avoid prejudice, discrimination, or stereotyping.

Covering may undermine the positive effects of a diverse and inclusive workplace and have an adverse effect on a person's feeling of authenticity. The work of DEIB is to cultivate a space where no one should feel the need to suppress parts of themselves that make them inherently who they are. Now there has to be some balance here. I often say that we have the right to be ourselves without imposing on someone else's right to do the same. One of the ways we are able to do so, to some extent, is through the legal parameters that preclude certain behaviors in public, such as lewdness, hate speech, and defamation. So when we talk about bringing our whole selves to work, the reality is that there are limitations to this. The goal should be to bring authenticity without the psychological weight to conform to a single narrative of what it means to be a valued member of an organization.

In conclusion, building a culture of DEIB advocacy requires support across the organization, especially from the top leadership team. If the senior leaders in your organization don't support DEIB initiatives, you are embarking on a fool's errand and will not only waste your time but may very well be putting your own well-being at risk because of the heaviness and emotional toll that comes with standing in the gap, so to speak. As noted earlier, it is important to engage employees in the various types of advocacy that draw their interest. Your team will also want to leverage as much data-driven insight as possible to help to both measure and monitor progress. Engagement surveys are helpful, as well as culture-specific assessments for solid baselines for continuous improvement. Finally, when considering a north star of transforming the organizational culture, keep in mind the vision highlighted in Fischer (2009) of the multicultural organization as envisaged by Cox, where "[t]he multi-cultural organization has 'full integration, structurally and informally, [and is] is free of bias and favoritism toward one group as compared with others, and has only a minimal intergroup conflict'" (p. 5). If you choose to embrace this ideal, what would you need to start, stop, or continue in order to achieve it?

References

Armenakis, A. A., Harris, S. G., and Mossholder, K. W. (1993). Creating readiness for organizational change. *Human Relations*, 46 (6), 681–709.

Bank of America (2023). https://about.bankofamerica.com/en/making-an-impact/racial-equality-economic-opportunity (archived at https://perma.cc/SDE8-54KV)

Bell, D. A. (1980). Brown v. Board of Education and the interest-convergence dilemma. *Harvard Law Review*, 93 (3), 518–33.

Blau, F. D. and Kahn, L. M. (2017). The gender wage gap: Extent, trends, and explanations. *Journal of Economic Literature*, 55 (3), 789–865.

Catalyst (2021). Inclusion: Action steps, www.catalyst.org/research/inclusion-action-steps/

Cox, T. H. and Blake, S. (1991). Managing cultural diversity: Implications for organizational competitiveness. *Academy of Management Perspectives*, 5 (3), 45–56.

Fischer, M. (2009). Diversity management and the business case. In K. Kraal, J. Roosblad, and J. Wrench (Eds.), *Equal Opportunities and Ethnic Inequality in European Labour Markets: Discrimination, Gender and Policies of Diversity* (pp. 95–118). Amsterdam University Press, http://www.jstor.org/stable/j.ctt46n0zz.8 (archived at https://perma.cc/WS8T-3VQE)

Gallup (2023, March 15). Research: Where employees think companies' DEIB efforts are failing. *Harvard Business Review*, https://hbr.org/2023/03/research-where-employees-think-companies-deib-efforts-are-failing (archived at https://perma.cc/P3R8-JPWP)

Gardenswartz, L. and Rowe, A. (1994). *Diverse Teams at Work: Capitalizing on the Power of Diversity*. Chicago, IL: Irwin Professional Publishing.

Gonzales, M. (2023). The psychological toll of 'covering' at work. SHRM, www.shrm.org/in/topics-tools/news/covering-at-work (archived at https://perma.cc/TN54-K87D)

IBM (2020) Diversity and Inclusion Report 2020, www.ibm.com/impact/be-equal/
pdf/IBM_Diversity_Inclusion_Report_2020.pdf (archived at https://perma.
cc/72AG-NXBD)

Kearney, E., Gebert, D., and Voelpel, S. (2009). When and how diversity benefits
teams: The importance of team members' need for cognition. *Academy of
Management Journal*, **52** (3), 581–98.

Kulik, C. T., Roberson, L., and Perry, E. L. (2007). The multiple-category problem:
Category activation and inhibition in the hiring process. *Academy of
Management Review*, **32** (2), 529–48.

McKinsey & Company. (2020). How diversity, equity, and inclusion (DE&I)
matter, www.mckinsey.com/featured-insights/diversity-and-inclusion/diversity-
wins-how-inclusion-matters (archived at https://perma.cc/R7VF-WMXX)

Mor Barak, M. E., Cherin, D. A., and Berkman, S. (1998). Organizational and
personal dimensions in diversity climate: Ethnic and gender differences in
employee perceptions. *Journal of Applied Behavioral Science*, **34** (1), 82–104.

Okun, T. (2001). *White Supremacy Culture*. DRworks.

Plaut, V. C., Garnett, F. G., Buffardi, L. E., and Sanchez-Burks, J. (2011). "What
about me?" Perceptions of exclusion and Whites' reactions to multiculturalism.
Journal of Personality and Social Psychology, **101** (2), 337.

Procter & Gamble (2023a). Engage, https://us.pg.com/take-on-race/engage/
(archived at https://perma.cc/4JUX-XCT5)

Procter & Gamble (2023b). Accelerating our supplier diversity efforts, https://
us.pg.com/blogs/pg-commits-to-spend-5-billion-with-diverse-owned-businesses/
(archived at https://perma.cc/9X8Y-YF8G)

Shore, L. M., Randel, A. E., Chung, B. G., Dean, M. A., Ehrhart, K. M., Singh, G.,
and Holcombe, K. M. (2011). Inclusion and diversity in work groups: A review
and model for future research. *Journal of Management*, **37** (4), 1262–89.

Target (2023) Racial equity action and change, https://corporate.target.com/
sustainability-governance/our-team/diversity-equity-inclusion/ racial-equity-
action-and-change (archived at https://perma.cc/6BVZ-XRFU)

Thomas, D. A. and Ely, R. J. (1996). Making differences matter: A new paradigm
for managing diversity. *Harvard Business Review*, **74** (5), 79–90.

U.S. Equal Employment Opportunity Commission (2007). 2007 EEO-1 national
aggregate report, http://www.eeoc.gov/eeoc/statistics/employment/jobpat-
eeo1/2007/us/national.html (archived at https://perma.cc/D5U6-DHUF)

4

Psychological Contracts

In the global economy there are organizations in a multitude of industries with a myriad of goals, some of which are anchored in capitalist ideologies, and others philanthropic. Peter Drucker (2001), the father of modern management and prominent business philosopher, said that creating customers is the goal of business, and that business has two basic functions: marketing and innovation. By contrast, nonprofit organizations are established to activate transformation in individuals and society (Drucker, 1990).

When someone decides to pursue a career, vocation, or job, the typical starting point is the role, then the kind of work to do, the company itself, and finally where the work will be done. Once the job offer is accepted, both the individual and the organization have a formal written contractual agreement on the work that will be done and when. However, there are also informal unwritten expectations from both parties. On the company side, the unwritten expectations are rooted in the organization's culture (norms, values, beliefs, ways of working). From the individual, those unwritten expectations are as unique as a fingerprint and can vary across industries and context. Nevertheless, unwritten expectations from both individuals and organizations can influence work experience in practical ways and form the essence of a *psychological contract*.

The concept of a psychological contract was developed in the1960s by organizational psychologist Chris Argyris and will likely be an enduring concept in the world of work for many years to come. Recent studies on employee work engagement tell us that when there are strong connections between the values of an individual and those of a company, employee engagement thrives. The work is not only more enjoyable, but the employees are also more effective and experience stronger organization commitment—the binding force between the individual and the organization. However, value sharing is often unidirectional until an employee is hired and surveyed to understand what they find important. Many companies share their values explicitly in published statements like internal policies and handbooks, as well as externally on websites, earnings, and annual reports.

The global Covid-19 pandemic created a seismic shift in the collective consciousness and for many elevated a desire for greater alignment with particular interests and values. Relocations increased, and remote work was the chosen approach. It's no surprise that a research study by the Society for Human Resource Management (Miller, 2022) revealed that across levels and industries, flexibility was the number one employee priority even for roles that couldn't be performed remotely. This demand led to companies rethinking and revamping their geographically bound hiring strategies, which provided two positive outcomes: increased employee retention and access to new talent. In the years following the pandemic some companies have retained hybrid and remote work policies, while others have transitioned back to in-office expectations. Two years post-pandemic, Goldman Sachs CEO David Solomon insisted on employees returning to the office five days a week, despite employees expressing feelings of being forced to come into the office and some threatening to quit due to the return-to-work policy. Since then, many companies have followed suit and are requiring employees to again work from an office space despite employee desire to continue hybrid or remote working arrangements. This is one of the more glaring examples of values misalignment that can happen over time between employees and organizations. In fact, we've seen quiet quitting and quiet firing, which may very well be the result of broken psychological contracts. At its core, this dynamic is a type of social exchange that has implications for employee engagement, retention, and ultimately business outcomes.

Unpacking Unspoken Employee Expectations

In an ideal world, it would be incredibly useful to have a comprehensive list of all the unspoken employee expectations, but the reality is that expectations can vary by industry and by role. For example, professionals working in the tech industry might expect the companies they work for to have the latest equipment available to do their work. Those who work in the arts might expect the freedom to express themselves in nontraditional ways. However, there a few relatively consistent themes around unspoken expectations that employees have of employers that have implications for engagement and retention. In fact, if there was a summary to encapsulate the themes, it is rooted in the difference between the advertised culture and the actual lived experiences. That said, the following themes tend to be enduring.

Work–life Balance

In 2022 Microsoft published results from the Work Trend Index survey they conducted using the independent research firm, Edelman Data x Intelligence. The survey asked questions of 31,102 full-time or self-employed workers across 31 markets between January 7, 2022 and February 16, 2022 and found five major themes:

- employees have a new "worth it" equation;
- managers feel wedged between leadership and employee expectations;
- leaders need to make the office worth the commute;
- flexible work doesn't have to mean "always on";
- rebuilding social capital looks different in a hybrid world.

The "worth it" equation is all about what employees want from their employers and what they are willing to do in exchange. Flexibility is part of the broader conversation around work-life balance, which is one of many unspoken employee expectations rooted in a desire for overall well-being. The morbid nature of the pandemic amplified this interest in supportive policies on mental health and caregiving responsibilities. The Microsoft study indicated young people were quitting because of well-being or mental health (24 percent), lack of work-life balance (24 percent) or because of a lack of flexibility in work hours or locations (21 percent). In fact, 47 percent of respondents said they were more likely to put family and personal life over work than they were before the pandemic, and 53 percent—particularly parents (55 percent) and women (56 percent)—said they were more likely to prioritize their health and well-being over work than before. Employees prioritizing their personal lives is a trend that's unlikely to shift any time soon. The expectation is that the organizations they work for will embrace flexibility and prioritize well-being.

Social Impact and International Policy Participation

For the multinational enterprise, participation in international policy is a process that requires strategic understanding of short- and long-term implications on operations worldwide. Corporate involvement in the political sphere has changed dramatically over the last half century, from reactive and defensive to a proactive, deliberate presence putting forward specific objectives to establish legitimacy in the countries in which they operate. Media reports are not without a constant barrage of content on corporate scandals related to policy violations in foreign operations management.

Operating a business internationally has costs and benefits that are often regulated by the peculiarities of sovereign governments that grant the use of and access to local resources needed to successfully execute operations. In fact, cross-border investments have tremendous implications on an organization's profitability and exposure to liability. Therefore, careful assessment of the risks and benefits of participation in international political policy is an imperative for the multinational enterprise. Across industries the prospect of increasing profitability, reducing liability, dominating market share, and improving shareholder value has convinced some organizations of the value of political participation.

Inherent to corporate involvement in political activity is quid pro quo: the benefits of international operations—including the return on investment in policy activities—must outweigh the costs. The landscape of involvement by corporate entities in the political sphere has changed dramatically over the last half century, shifting from companies being reactive and defensive, with a desire to remain off the government's radar, to a front-and-center proactive presence putting forward specific objectives.

In the United States in particular, corporate lobbying has influenced policies and practices in favor of companies with significant financial resources. Lobbying can be public or private and correspondingly transparent or opaque. The use of corporate PACs and lobbying are said to be among the most important political activities companies can be involved with. Often, lobbying is perceived by business leaders to have a potential positive impact on revenues. The decisions organizations make about involvement in political activity are shaped largely by the personal ideologies of the executive leader. If a CEO holds an ideology about potential payoffs from specific policies and regulations, those areas are most likely to be lobbied the most. Leaders of organizations often use a combination of lobbying and campaign contributions to impact the political climate affecting the organization. In the United States there is oversight of donations related to lobbying, and firms that engage in lobbying outperform organizations that do not.

In some extreme cases, corporate political involvement can lead to market-closing advantages that could eliminate competition. Depending on the point of view, this can be both an advantage and disadvantage. Boddewyn and Brewer (1994) assert that involvement with "governments can also generate 'unnatural' market imperfections through the granting of monopoly privileges, preferential access to scarce resources, involvement in public policy making and other means" (p. 134). Moreover, the risks are even higher for smaller firms. "[S]ome feel under-represented... others worry that they are being used as pawns" (The Economist, 2012). In fact, there is no guarantee that the investment in political activity will yield a favorable outcome, but given these strong financial incentives for corporate involvement in political action in both domestic and international contexts, we are unlikely to see a reduction in these efforts in the foreseeable future.

An example of a global company that has succeeded in collaborating with multiple local stakeholders is PepsiCo. In a speech given at the 2014 BSR Conference on sustainability, Indra Nooyi, then Chairman and CEO of PepsiCo, discussed how the business collaborated with communities and agricultural organizations in India to improve water conservation. One of PepsiCo's goals was to improve access to water for residents in communities in which they were operating. As a result, the business became more profitable, more efficient, and reduced their environmental impact. Moreover, PepsiCo has maintained a license to do business in India since 2009 (Nooyi, 2014). PepsiCo's approach was brilliant in that the business recognized that short-term profitability was not as important as sustainability efforts with long-term implications in the communities where they operated. Corporate political actions by PepsiCo created win-win outcomes that contributed to securing future business in the region.

How to begin? With an ever-changing global economy, companies with multinational operations are challenged to consider the costs and benefits of international policy participation. Depending on the firm size, business goals, budget for political actions, and associated risks, participation in corporate political policy activities "makes sense only when benefits exceed costs" (Boddewyn and Brewer, 1994, p. 133). Getting involved in political activities does not guarantee favorable outcomes, although risk and cost can be mitigated through collaborations with third-party specialty groups or by joining efforts with firms that have similar interests.

However, when considering how to begin corporate political involvement, organizations should first identify whom within the company will represent its interests to a group or government entity. With the appropriate representative established, the company can focus on developing relationships with local government agencies by making a good faith effort to understand the workforce development and community needs of the places where they operate. Once these needs are understood, the next step is committing to finding win-win solutions that have the potential to increase social capital.

Relationship building may very well be the key to gaining the respect and support needed by multinational firms to enter the realm of political policy. Although quid pro quo might still exist, how local legislators respond to the needs of the multinational company could shift in favor of international organizations when they demonstrate a commitment to true corporate social responsibility.

It is hard to imagine doing business in isolation in any region of the world without visibility, expectations, and criticism from some interested parties. From an employee's expectation, social engagement, participation, accountability, and responsibility are akin to a competitive salary.

Commitments to Diversity and Inclusion

On May 25, 2020, the tragedy surrounding George Floyd's death was recorded and shared on social media, spawning a global outrage about police brutality and racial injustice. Many organizations were compelled to respond, or risk being "cancelled" for lack of engagement. Promises were made and commitments were published:

- Google pledged to invest $1 billion in racial equity over the next five years. Current commitments include helping to create economic opportunity, improving education, and supporting racial justice organizations.
- Nike committed to hiring 50,000 Black employees by 2025. They also pledged to invest $100 million in Black businesses and communities.
- Target announced that it would be donating $10 million to organizations working to advance racial justice.

Many organizations pledged to increase the representation of marginalized people in their leadership positions. There were also commitments to change policies and culture, which included hiring roles that focused on diversity, equity, inclusion, and belonging initiatives. However, not all companies followed through on their commitments, and in recent years some have pulled back completely and have gone so far as to eliminate roles such as Chief Diversity

Officer. This is one example of an implicit expectation of employees to have their employers engage in initiatives that have a social impact.

There is also an expectation around inclusive leadership, whereby employees have a say in the way things are done in an organization. More progressive institutions may have mechanisms to capture the feedback and insights from employees, while other companies have more traditional approaches to capture employee interests by way of engagement surveys. At the core of these desires is the notion of amplifying the voices of those who do not typically have a say or those who are often marginalized.

Opportunity for Growth and Job Security

It may come as no surprise that many job applicants choose a company based on what they believe it can do for their career. Once they join, employees often have implicit expectations for support toward advancement in their careers and the continuity of stability. They are interested in receiving training, professional development, mentoring, and having clear paths for promotion.

These expectations can look slightly different for various generations. In a similar vein there are also expectations of receiving meaningful work that is directly connected to areas of personal or professional interest, coupled with autonomy and high impact.

What most employees lack insight into is that leading organizations often determine the talent management strategies most appropriate to sustain and develop their business objectives. Comprehensive talent management often includes areas such as candidate selection, development, and reward systems, in addition to competency management, performance management, succession planning, and aspects of diversity. In fact, when discussing talent management, it is important to note that "there is no single or universal contemporary definition of 'talent' in any one language; there are different organizational perspectives of talent, [and] current meanings of talent tend to be specific to an organization and highly influenced by the nature of the work undertaken" (Tansley, 2011, p. 266). Furthermore, "organizations find greater value in formulating their own meaning of what talent is than accepting universal or prescribed definitions. So there will be considerable differences in how talent is defined in a local authority, a trans-national organization and a small enterprise" (Tansley, 2011, p. 270).

It should be noted that "only when individuality resonates strongly with the organizational ideal does it stand a chance of being recognized and praised as talent" (Swailes, 2013, p. 36). Although organizations may take different approaches to talent management based on the business definition, "a common notion of organizational talent refers to those who are identified as having the potential to reach high levels of achievement" (Tansley, 2011, p. 266).

Talent management efforts are often costly and time consuming due to the resources needed to identify and screen potential new hires. Although many organizations are meticulous in their talent planning, the level of consideration given to ethical approaches to selection and development programs is unclear. "A core question in considering the ethics of employment is how far do employers have moral responsibilities to care for their employees? Care embodies a range of factors such as a safe working environment free from discrimination along with decent working conditions and fair remuneration" (Swailes, 2013, p. 37). What might be more interesting to employees is the fact that there are differentiated programs called *high-potential programs* for career advancement in organizations that aren't typically discussed openly.

Vloeberghs, Pepermans and Thielemans (2005) offer insights that the content of high-potential development programs are different from what is offered to other managers. The former have dedicated more time and offer a broader set of vertical and horizontal activities. These initiatives are designed to identify, recruit, develop, and provide accelerated management and leadership opportunities (Derr et al., 1988; Harris and Feild, 1992; Kotter, 1990).

Kotter (1990) states, "Especially talented and ambitious individuals often move up these narrow hierarchies at great speed" (p. 120). Some managers may be reluctant to give significant work knowing that these employees may not be in position for an extended period of time. As a consequence, moving through jobs every 12 to 18 months does not allow an opportunity for in-depth learning, or an understanding of the results of their actions (Kotter, 1990). Furthermore, rapid job rotation can instill an understanding of short-sighted management but very little about leadership (Kotter, 1990).

Dalziel (2004) discusses the ways high-potential leaders present themselves as leaders and highlights three important attributes that should be sought in this group: self-confidence and self-awareness, an ability to objectively evaluate situations and others, and possession of emotional fortitude, all of which are balanced and constant (Dalziel, 2004). The question becomes, how diverse are these programs? And are there objective measures for selection? Furthermore, what can the average employee do to get access to these programs and opportunities for rapid advancement? Well, there is no guarantee that your company has these programs so I wouldn't bank on it. However, exceptional performance outcomes are key differen-tiators for financial rewards and promotions in most companies, and there are general career paths for most job functions. The proactive employee would do well to discuss their career aspirations with their human resources business partner and direct manager to understand what it would take to get to a particular level in the company as a means of creating an individual development plan as a way forward.

Trust and Integrity

Future employees and financial investors consider the reputation of an organization at the onset before making any formal engagement for employment or collaboration. Oftentimes there are explicit expecta-tions around integrity within an organization that are drafted in policies or even captured in mission statements. Some of the most common statements around trust and integrity are laid out in data protection and privacy statements that many of us have received when signing up to various service providers. Employees have implicit and explicit expectations that their data privacy will be managed with integrity. Employment applications often require demographic data like gender, race, Social Security number, and previous salaries, and Human Resource and IT teams collaborate to secure employee information. However, integrity and trust extend far beyond baseline expectations around data protection. Employees expect leaders, managers, and fellow colleagues to follow through on their commitments. For example, during times of economic hardship when businesses are making difficult decisions around employee headcount, leaders should exercise tremendous caution around what the business will or will not do. Employees as well as external stakeholders expect the leaders' communicated intention to align with current and future actions. Some examples of companies that lost trust with employees, and the general public for that matter, include Wells Fargo, Uber, Facebook, and Theranos.

WELLS FARGO

In 2016, Wells Fargo Bank violated the trust of millions of potential customers when they opened a number of accounts in their names without their authorization. The Consumer Financial Protection Bureau fined the bank millions of dollars for taking this unauthorized action. There are several challenges that this case presents as it relates to trust and integrity. On the one hand there was a culture within Wells Fargo that rewarded and facilitated these unscrupulous practices that otherwise went unpunished. On the other hand, the actions taken by Wells Fargo employees to open these accounts without the authorization of their customers violated their trust. The backlash was fierce and customers were infuriated; 5,300 employees were fired and Wells Fargo was fined $185 million for opening fraudulent accounts and required to refund customers approximately $5 million. Four years later, in one of the final investigations and as part of a three-year deferred prosecution agreement, Wells Fargo was required to pay the United States Justice Department and Securities and Exchange Commission $3 billion to resolve the fraudulent sales practices that the bank encouraged with their unrealistic sales goals and pressuring employees in creating fake accounts between 2002 and 2016. The unfortunate truth here is that Wells Fargo successfully cultivated a culture lacking integrity and rewarded that lack of integrity.

UBER

In 2017, Uber dominated the news headlines due to a series of corporate scandals that included allegations of sexual harassment, discrimination, and the unfortunate fatal car crash that involved one of their self-driving cars. As a result, then CEO Travis Kalanick resigned, and the year after joining Uber as their chief brand officer, Bozoma Saint John also resigned (Miller, 2019). It was not until her appearance at the South by Southwest Festival in 2019 that the public received insights into her short tenure with Uber. During the Q&A session Saint John revealed her desire to be an agent of change for women and people of color at Uber. However, her experience proved to be an overwhelming one and she concluded that she didn't need to be the savior.

The spotlight on Uber garnered an investigation which resulted in the firing of 20 employees, including some senior executives. In 2019 the US Equal Employment Opportunity Commission, also known as the EEOC, which has a mission to "prevent and remedy unlawful employment discrimination and advance equal opportunity for all in the workplace," concluded that Uber's culture permitted both sexual harassment and retaliation. As a result the company was said to have paid $4.4 million to employees who had experienced harassment in the workplace.

FACEBOOK

The use of social media has become ubiquitous in our modern age. Platforms are leveraged to share updates on day-to-day activities, reflections on current events, or even to provide guidance and insights to others. With this level of sharing, the expectation for privacy is naïve, but in some regions of the world, like the European Union, there are opportunities for social media users to remove/delist certain personal information that comes up in queries on platforms like Google by way of "right to be forgotten" legislation established in 2014. Even with this baseline understanding, nothing could have prepared Facebook users for the bombshell data breach that allowed what could be described as the ultimate Svengali-led social engineering endeavor for political positioning. In 2018, a whistleblower from the political consulting firm Cambridge Analytica revealed that in 2014, 87 million Facebook profiles worldwide had been accessed without user consent to build targeted political ads.

Facebook CEO Mark Zuckerberg was brought before the United States Congress to answer questions on this data breach and allowing the ads to run on Facebook. After an investigation, Facebook was fined £500,000 by the United Kingdom's Information Commissioner Office. Although they agreed to pay the fine, as part of the deal Facebook made no admission of liability and were allowed to keep certain documents from being disclosed. The Federal Trade Commission (FTC) in the United States fined Facebook $5 billion, in part for deceiving users into believing they had a certain level of agency over their ability to control their privacy. The settlement also required Facebook to create a new privacy structure and the development of new tools for the FTC to monitor Facebook directly. Although the business made changes to policies connected to the information that developers can access, and parameters for users to protect their personal information, the loss of trust resulted in many users deleting their accounts. According to the Securities and Exchange Commission complaint, in September 2015, some Facebook employees attempted to highlight concerns about Cambridge Analytica (Lomas, 2019). Those concerns went ignored. One can only imagine the domino effect on the political landscape if had not been.

THERANOS

This healthcare startup wasn't quite a household name until it took the spotlight due to fraud. Founded in 2003, Theranos raised $700 million and soon secured partnerships with the likes of Cleveland Clinic and Safeway for what was thought to be an innovation in blood testing and diagnosis. The culture was rooted in secrecy and control. However, that did not prevent scientists working for the company in the early development phase from cautioning against a public offering of the technology due to inaccuracies with test results. After investigations by regulators like the Federal Drug Administration in the United States, it was found that Theranos testing technology was indeed inaccurate. What's even more disturbing was the discovery that Theranos had be using traditional testing approaches provided by other testing companies. That's like opening a bakery that claims to sell freshly baked bread but in reality actually buying supermarket shelf bread and selling it as your own.

By 2018, the Securities and Exchange Commission charged Elizabeth Holmes, the company founder, with fraud, and in May of 2023, Holmes reported to a minimum-security prison in Texas to begin her 11-year sentence. Holmes's actions in creating a business rooted in fraud put the public at risk with inaccurate blood testing results and cost investors not only financially but in social capital and trust. Had Holmes and her investors taken more time to develop the technology, they might have realized what they purported. Instead, they chose deceit and cutting corners, putting lives at risk.

Any employee walking into an environment that has been riddled with controversy and high levels of turnover in leadership could potentially experience a significant trepidation around the future of the business as well as a lack of trust until stability and consistency enable the development and renewing of trust in the broader organization system. When employees see other employees performing certain tasks in a particular way that does not align to ethical practices and those behaviors go unpunished and without accountability, the implicit and explicit expectations around the way work gets done create a level of comfort to continue to either ignore or participate in unscrupulous practices.

Rebuilding trust starts with admitting the wrongs that were done and transparency around those missteps. With the help of internal team members and neutral external third parties, organizations can create measures of accountability and explicit changes in policy commitments to lay a new foundation for building culture grounded in ethical practices.

Fair Treatment

Fair and equitable treatment is yet another expectation from many who join organizations. Fairness can encompass a number of things, including compensation, rewards for performance, as well as opportunities for growth and promotion. The issues of fairness tend to be more heightened around the time of year when employees are rewarded for the prior year's performance. Issues such as pay transparency tend to come up, as well as complaints around fair compensation, or appropriate recognition for various work that was accomplished during the year.

Defining what is fair is an interesting endeavor. For example, there have been companies, although few and far between, that opted to pay every employee the exact same salary, irrespective of experience and education. We've also seen and are aware of what appeared to be exorbitant salaries for senior-level executives at publicly traded companies. However, beyond these extremes, there is some type of middle ground. In fact, most organizations tend to hire specialists within the field of compensation and benefits to benchmark and validate a balanced approach to salary offerings, and ensure that employees are compensated according to their experience and education, as well as what the organization can afford for a given role. When it comes to recognition for contributions through performance appraisals, it's always helpful when an organization has a transparent way of evaluating performance. For example, if there is a clear rubric that describes the behaviors and outcomes, in other words, the "what" and a "how" of a given performance rating, that is very helpful to employees to understand the ways in which they will be evaluated. However, when an organization has unclear or ambiguous expectations, this can be either misinterpreted or leveraged in ways that are unbalanced, and employees are not provided with the kind of insight needed to predict where they would land in terms of their performance outcomes.

It's also important that there are goals. Ironically, not all organizations allow employees to align their day-to-day work with specific goals, and by goals I mean what is commonly referred to in the management literature as management by objectives or MBOs. When objectives are outlined, and goals are clear and defined, both the employee and the manager have an opportunity to monitor progress toward those goals over a specific timeframe. There are also opportunities for course correction if there is a recognition that a goal may not be achieved for some reason—for example, changes in the market limits to resources—again, creating that level of predictability that can indeed create a sense of fairness and balance in the performance appraisals and evaluation. The other challenge with performance evaluations is the measures used to determine promotion or advancement. For example, ability and awareness of contributions are typical factors that can go into an individual's consideration for promotion.

Respectful and Supportive Work Environment

It goes without saying that people expect their work environment to be free from harassment and discrimination, and full of support and respect. Most organizations have a legal obligation to provide such a space for colleagues to do their best work. Therefore, hiring and training employees to align their behaviors to cultivate inclusive outcomes is essential. One of the ways companies can go beyond baseline legal obligations is in outlining principles and values around ways of working. These can serve as guideposts on expectations and create clarity for performance outcomes.

That said, there is an elaborate dance of expectations that goes on within the ostensibly hard boundaries of an organization. Psychological contracts are unspoken agreements that connect employers and employees in a web of reciprocal duties, going beyond formal written contracts. These unspoken agreements, which are formed by implicit understandings and changing perceptions, have a significant impact on the success of organizations, employee engagement, and personal well-being. The views, expectations, and ideas that workers have about the conditions of their connection with the company and its representatives define psychological contracts. These agreements, which are developed through a combination of explicit agreements, implicit commitments, and experiences within the organization, are not overtly expressed. They cover a wide range of topics, including work-life balance, career development prospects, job security, and the general work environment.

An essential indicator of corporate success, employee engagement is directly impacted by the strength of the psychological contract. Strong contracts that are based on open communication, mutual trust, and met expectations encourage employees' intrinsic drive. They put forth more effort, are more creative, and are more devoted to their work because they feel respected, in control, and committed to it. On the other hand, a breach of contract, which is characterized by unmet expectations, unjust treatment, or broken promises, causes disengagement and shows up as rising absenteeism, decreased productivity, and eventually high turnover rates. Because psychological contracts and engagement are directly correlated, it is clear how important they are for creating a positive corporate culture.

Psychological contracts have an impact on an organization's overall health in addition to individual participation. Employees report better mental health and higher job satisfaction when they believe they are treated fairly and that their efforts are valued. Positive spillover effects improve communication, create collaborative work environments, and improve dispute resolution in the workplace. On the other hand, a poor contract might encourage negativity, mistrust, and emotional dissonance, which will harm everyone at work by creating a toxic environment. Psychological contracts play a pivotal role in determining employee satisfaction and motivation levels within organizations. When employees feel that the organization is fulfilling its obligations and meeting their expectations they experience higher job satisfaction. This in turn leads to increased motivation levels, productivity, and commitment toward organizational goals.

On the other hand, when psychological contract breaches occur, such as unfulfilled promises or inconsistent treatment, employee satisfaction and motivation decline, resulting in decreased productivity and increased turnover rates. Employee loyalty and devotion to the company are greatly influenced by psychological contracts. People are more inclined to be loyal to an organization when they believe that their psychological contract is being upheld. They show better levels of corporate civic behavior and become more invested in their work, often going above and beyond. On the other hand, when psychological contract violations happen, staff members can feel deceived, lowering their commitment and loyalty and hurting the performance of the company as a whole. Therefore, employee satisfaction depends not only on performance reviews, but also the overall culture of the company.

Psychological contracts, however, are dynamic agreements that are always changing as a result of continuing interactions and experiences rather than static texts. Changes in leadership, organizational structures, or even personal circumstances can reshape expectations and rewrite the parameters of the implicit agreement. It is in these moments of change and reassessment that proactive management and open communication are essential. Leaders need to be proactive in addressing employee concerns, promoting open communication, and showing that they are committed to keeping their half of the agreement. Embracing open communication and realizing the dynamic nature of these contracts helps firms manage challenging periods while preserving great employee relationships.

Getting Through the Obstacles

Despite their significance, addressing and sustaining psychological contracts is not easy. Unrealistic expectations can cause frustration and unhappiness in both employers and employees. For example, unanticipated events like economic downturns or restructuring may call for adjustments that could be interpreted as violations of the terms of the contract. In these kinds of circumstances, trust-building techniques like open communication, empathy, and a readiness to renegotiate become essential. Organizations may effectively manage challenging situations and preserve great relationships with their valued human capital by recognizing the difficulties and taking a proactive approach.

Summary

Several studies have shown that breaches in psychological contracts negatively impact job satisfaction, lead to disruptive behaviors, and increase employee turnover intention. Taking intentional steps to understand employee expectations can help companies better manage those expectations and potentially improve retention and organization performance. Some areas to give attention to beyond competitive compensation are having a positive culture, mental health/well-being benefits, a sense of purpose/meaning, flexible work hours, more than the standard two weeks of paid vacation time each year, positive feedback and recognition, and career advancement.

At the end of the day, psychological contracts are not just an afterthought in the context of organizations; rather, they are the treasures that could promote well-being, engagement, and eventually, organizational success. Organizations have the power to change the narrative from one of silent expectations to one of open communication, respect, and shared commitment by acknowledging the importance of psychological contracts and making investments in their upkeep. By doing this, they open the door to a future in which employers and employees not only get along but actually flourish together thanks to an imperceptible but strong relationship of reciprocal duties. This change in viewpoint—from transactional ties to meaningful contracts—has the power to fundamentally alter organizational life and foster an environment where both individual and group development are cultivated.

To build and preserve productive working relationships, psychological contracts are essential for employers and employees. They have a major effect on retention rates, motivation, and employee satisfaction in businesses. Through successful management of psychological contracts and fulfillment of responsibilities, firms can foster a healthy work environment, increase employee engagement, lower attrition rates, and establish a great employer brand. Understanding the significance of psychological contracts is crucial for companies hoping to succeed over the long haul in the cutthroat world of business today.

References

Boddewyn, J. J. and Brewer, T. L. (1994). International-business political behavior: New theoretical directions. *The Academy of Management Review*, **19** (1), 119–43.

Dalziel, M. M. (2004). Determining every employee's potential for growth. In L. Berger and D. Berger (Eds.), *The Talent Management Handbook: Creating Organizational Excellence by Identifying, Developing, and Promoting Your Best People*, 129–38. New York, London: McGraw-Hill.

Derr, C. B., Jones, C., and Toomey, E. L. (1988). Managing high-potential employees: Current practices in thirty-three U.S. corporations. *Human Resources Management*, **21** (3), 273–90.

Drucker, P. F. (1990). *Managing the Nonprofit Organization: Principles and Practices*. HarperCollins Publishers.

Drucker, P. F. (2001). *The Essential Drucker*. CollinsBusiness.

The Economist (2012) The chamber of secrets. http://www.economist.com/node/21553020 (archived at https://perma.cc/E6NU-QN5R)

Harris, S. G. and Feild, H. S. (1992). Realizing the potential of high-potential management development programmes. *Journal of Management Development*, **11** (1), 61–70.

Kotter, J. P. (1990). *A Force for Change: How Leadership Differs from Management*. New York: Free Press.

Lomas, N. (2019). Facebook ignored staff warnings about "sketchy" Cambridge Analytica in September 2015. TechCrunch, https://techcrunch.com/2019/07/25/facebook-ignored-staff-warnings-about-sketchy-cambridge-analytica-in-september-2015/ (archived at https://perma.cc/4ZPK-LPG7)

Microsoft (2022) Great Expectations: Making Hybrid Work *Work*, www.microsoft.com/en-us/worklab/work-trend-index/great-expectations-making-hybrid-work-work (archived at https://perma.cc/324A-E8XM)

Miller, J. (2019) Bozom Saint John explains why she left Uber, *Variety*, https://variety.com/2019/biz/news/bozoma-saint-john-leaving-uber-apple-endeavor-1203162824/ (archived at https://perma.cc/SCA9-7VBW)

Miller, S. (2022). Priorities shift as pandemic recedes, SHRM 2022 Employee Benefit Survey shows. SHRM, www.shrm.org/resourcesandtools/hr-topics/benefits/pages/benefits-priorities-shift-as-the-pandemic-recedes-shrm-2022-employee-benefits-survey-shows.aspx (archived at https://perma.cc/B7XU-FAF5)

Nooyi, I. (2014, November 11). BSR conference 2014: Indra Nooyi, chairman and CEO Pepsico www.youtube.com/watch?v=iicVUa8bANA (archived at https://perma.cc/9GU9-KYKD)

Swailes, S. (2013). The ethics of talent management. *Business Ethics: A European Review*, **22** (1), 32–46.

Tansley, C. (2011). What do we mean by the term "talent" in talent management? *Industrial and Commercial Training*, **43** (5), 266–74.

U.S. Equal Employment Opportunity Commission (2019) www.eeoc.gov/overview (archived at https://perma.cc/Z86Q-VF94)

Vloeberghs, D., Pepermans, R., and Thielemans, K. (2005). High-potential developmentpolicies: an empirical study among Belgian companies. *Journal of Management Development*, **24** (6), 546–58.

5

Psychological Safety

Psychological safety as a construct stems from research focused on organizational change by Schein and Bennis in the 1960s: "They described it as the extent to which individuals feel secure and confident in their ability to manage change" (Newman, Donohue, and Eva, 2017, p. 523). Over the years, other researchers have focused on the study of psychological safety in the workplace. One of the more popular conceptualizations of psychological safety came through the work of Amy Edmondson in the late 1990s, who defined it as the "shared belief held by members of a team that the team is safe for interpersonal risk taking" (Edmondson, 1999, p. 350). In a 2023 article published by global management consulting firm, McKinsey, psychological safety is described as "the absence of interpersonal fear" (McKinsey, 2023).

The psychological safety of employees is a powerful force that exists beneath the visible structures and established processes of an organization's day-to-day operations. Different from physical safety, this elusive idea explores the emotional and cognitive sphere and shapes people's perceptions of their workplace. Psychological safety is more than just comfort; it creates an atmosphere that allows growth, ideas to bloom, and vulnerabilities to be accepted.

The idea of psychological safety has become important in the study of organizational psychology. It alludes to the team members' common conviction that they can take chances in their relationships with others without worrying about how it will affect their status or job. People can openly communicate their ideas, worries, and views in this secure space, which promotes cooperation and confidence. The purpose of this chapter is to examine the significance of psychological safety in the workplace and how it affects workers' productivity, well-being, and creativity. In order to foster a supportive work atmosphere where people feel free to be themselves and voice their thoughts, psychological safety is essential. People are more prone to conceal important input when they fear judgment, criticism, or punishment for voicing their opinions. This leads to wasted possibilities for creativity and progress. Edmondson (1999) asserts that workplaces that support psychological safety foster candid dialogue, active engagement, and constructive criticism, all of which increase worker satisfaction and engagement.

Fundamentally, psychological safety is the conviction that, because of a relationship based on trust and respect, people can take interpersonal risks without worrying about the consequences. It's a feeling of safety fostered by a welcoming atmosphere in which raising one's voice, voicing disagreements in a constructive way, and even making mistakes are seen as necessary steps toward group growth and learning rather than as crimes to be punished. People can let go of their inhibitions, be true to themselves, and share their own viewpoints without having to self-censor since they are no longer afraid. What is the outcome? An active environment that fosters creativity, teamwork, and problem-solving and that unleashes the full potential of the human intellect.

A culture of psychological safety is not achieved in a straight line; rather, it is the result of constant learning, adjustment, and improvement. There will be difficulties and disappointments, but there are unquestionably huge potential rewards. By embracing this revolutionary idea, organizations set out to fully utilize their human resources, promoting a feeling of unity and well-being among all members of the organization. In time, we can aspire to a space where work will no longer be seen as a mere transaction but rather as an environment that fosters development, creativity, and the blooming of the human spirit. In a utopia, psychological safety acts as the unseen foundation upon which both individuals and organizations might construct a more engaging human-centered work experience.

Moreover, creating a culture of psychological safety must be established with purpose and deliberate effort. To set the tone, leadership must be vulnerable, promote open communication, and actively seek out different viewpoints. The safety net created is further strengthened by fostering a feedback culture where learning is promoted and constructive criticism is valued. Building psychological trust is essential for maintaining this fragile ecology. It can be achieved through openness and regular fulfillment of commitments. By implementing these tactics, companies may create an environment where psychological safety thrives, and people are empowered to enjoy the benefits of a genuinely engaged and productive workforce.

Enabling people to thrive is the true goal of psychological safety, not simply to shield them from harm. People feel secure to push themselves beyond their comfort zones when they are in an atmosphere that accepts vulnerability and views mistakes as teaching moments. This builds resilience, empowering people to overcome obstacles, adjust to change, and develop from trying circumstances. On the other hand, a lack of psychological safety can cause stress, worry, and disengagement, endangering the well-being of workers and impeding their ability to advance professionally. Organizations that prioritize psychological safety make investments in their employees' long-term well-being and professional advancement in addition to their current performance.

To sum it up, psychological safety goes beyond the dispassionate computation of measurements and figures. It explores the human experience of work and cultivates a setting where people feel comfortable, respected, and empowered to reach their full potential. Organizations that give priority to this elusive component open a treasure chest of advantages, from improved resilience and employee well-being to increased creativity. This paradigm change—from a transactional to a human-centered approach—is not only a sentimental endeavor; it is essential to the long-term success of organizations and their ability to grow sustainably.

Psychological safety has positive effects on an organization's external stakeholders in addition to its internal benefits. Stronger customer service translates into increased brand loyalty and market share when employees feel empowered and engaged. Furthermore, companies that put a high priority on ethical behavior and the well-being of their workers draw and keep top talent, which helps them stand out in the competitive market. A culture of psychological safety has an impact on the community and shapes a more responsible and healthier corporate ecosystem well beyond the confines of the office.

In a world where upheaval and uncertainty are the norm, it is not only possible but also imperative to promote psychological safety. It is a call to action for leaders in all fields to rethink corporate cultures, shifting from hierarchies based on fear and control to ones based on vulnerability, trust, and mutual development. It will need bravery, commitment, and a readiness to accept a human-centric approach to leadership to make this change. Leaders need to set a good example by aggressively tearing down organizational walls, promoting candid dialogue, and valuing different points of view.

Setting psychological safety as a top priority is an investment in the future as well as the present. Organizations create an environment that is conducive to long-term success by providing a secure space for people to grow, learn, and innovate. In the long run, they ensure their relevance and competitiveness by providing their workforce with the resilience and agility needed to manage the ever-shifting marketplace. Organizations that value the human experience and foster psychological safety as a cornerstone will surely attract and keep the greatest people, setting themselves up for success in a world where talent is the most important resource.

A key component of developing a productive workplace where workers may flourish and contribute to the success of the company is psychological safety. It encourages candid communication, boosts worker satisfaction, encourages innovation and creativity, and strengthens teamwork. Businesses that place a high priority on psychological safety are better able to draw in and keep top personnel, promote a culture of ongoing learning and development, and adjust to the constantly shifting needs of the market. Organizations can help people reach their full potential and achieve sustainable growth and success by understanding the value of psychological safety and putting strategies in place to foster it.

Over time, psychological safety has been a topic that has obtained more prominence, especially in the social media space, as it relates to creating an environment where people of color can thrive. In layman's terms, feeling psychologically safe is essentially having a sense that the things that one chooses to say, or ways in which someone might choose to show up, would be welcomed. There's also the sentiment that an individual would not be punished for sharing ideas or ridiculed for providing a perspective that does not necessarily align with the ways those in a racial or other representative majority might view the world. So, the question becomes: Why should we even bother to think about this as something organizations should be concerned about?

Psychological safety is the unseen glue that holds teams together. It promotes psychological cohesiveness, in which free communication and trust are accepted as the norm. People are at ease asking for assistance, disclosing worries, and sharing victories with one another. Better communication, a deeper feeling of purpose, and improved team performance are all results of this collaborative mentality. On the other hand, a lack of psychological safety damages team relationships and impedes advancement by encouraging mistrust, loneliness, and an "every man for himself" mentality. Organizations can develop high-performing teams that accomplish more than the sum of their individual parts by fostering this sense of collective security.

Employees who work in a psychologically safe atmosphere are less stressed, anxious, or burned out. Their mental health and general well-being are positively impacted by feeling respected and supported. According to a 1999 study by Spreitzer et al., workers who feel more psychologically safe at work report better general psychological health, lower levels of job-related stress, and higher levels of job satisfaction. Through a decrease in absenteeism and turnover rates, these favorable results not only benefit the workforce but also advance organizational performance.

Teams that function in a psychologically secure atmosphere exhibit increased levels of cooperation, trust, and unity. Decision-making and problem-solving procedures are enhanced when team members feel comfortable asking for and receiving support, as well as sharing their opinions. According to a 2002 study by Edmondson, teams with psychological safety demonstrate higher levels of learning, knowledge sharing, and creativity, which improves team performance and productivity.

Psychological safety not only fosters a comfortable work environment but also ignites the creative and innovative spark. Myriad viewpoints arise when people feel comfortable speaking out about their beliefs, no matter how outlandish they may sound. This cross-pollination of ideas produces groundbreaking solutions, encourages risk-taking, and advances organizations in a setting that is changing quickly. Conversely, a lack of psychological safety in the workplace discourages innovation, which breeds conformity and stifles potentially revolutionary ideas. Organizations that put psychological safety first therefore benefit from an innovative culture that helps them advance in the competition.

Furthermore, employees are more inclined to engage in diverse thinking, explore new options, and challenge the status quo when they feel free to voice their opinions and take calculated risks without worrying about the repercussions. Employees who feel psychologically protected are more likely to solve problems creatively, which produces original ideas and solutions. This encourages an innovative and flexible culture that helps businesses remain competitive in the fast-changing business environment of today.

In my mind, psychological safety is akin to the freedom to be and express your full self within the environment in which you are engaging. Therefore, when someone is psychologically safe, they are essentially free. Now imagine that you are tasked with both coming up with a new idea and also evaluating current practices. When you think about it, you believe that you possess the skills and abilities needed to adequately evaluate the current systems and offerings, and that you possess sufficient creativity and insight to offer a new solution. With that level of confidence, the things you would choose to say, and the way you might go about your evaluation, would be significantly different than if you walked into the scenario with trepidation or concerns around how your ideas might be received. This is the essence of imposter syndrome, which can create a sentiment that one does not belong or does not possess the ability to do something, even when they do.

In recent years, there's been a lot of talk about how to create an environment for employees to feel welcomed and comfortable bringing their full self to work. This is a very a challenging ask for many reasons. First, it takes tremendous courage to come into a business environment, showing up with all aspects of one's intersectional identities. Second, companies are not prepared to support what it means to have their employees engage colleagues as their full selves. The workplace has never really been a place that has invited differences. In fact, what we have seen most often is a desire for alignment and connection to what is known and familiar, which historically has not been diverse.

Let's take the CROWN Act for example, which is a law that was passed in July 2019 in some US states to prevent discrimination against people of color who choose to wear their hair in traditional styles. People of color can have hair textures that range from naturally straight to tightly coiled curls. In recent years we've seen a proliferation of media clips in the United States and even South Africa, primarily in school settings, where students of color have been either asked to change their hair styles to reflect the dominant culture expectations or face consequences such as losing access to a given activity, or the right to participate in a graduation ceremony.

Due to his refusal to alter his haircut, Darryl George, a Black student at a Texas high school, was sent to in-school suspension. This action reignited a months-long dispute over a clothing rule that the teen's family views as discriminatory. Darryl was given a 13-day suspension for not wearing his hair down, as stated in a disciplinary notification from Barbers Hill High School in Mont Belvieu, Texas. He had been attending an off-site disciplinary program for a month, and this was his first day back at the school. His braided locks, which dropped below his eyebrows and ear lobes, were reported to have violated the district's dress code, which led to his initial removal from the classroom at the Houston-area school in August, according to school authorities. His family claims the penalty is against the Texas

CROWN Act, which went into effect in September 2023 and forbids discrimination based on race in hairstyles. The school claims that hair length is not addressed by the CROWN Act (Associated Press, 2023).

The dominant narrative is that these hairstyles are unprofessional. When compared to what is deemed professional, the contrasting hairstyles are Eurocentric in appearance. Most of those hair styles are modeled by individuals that have straight or wavy texture, and the styles are subdued and restrained, either in a bun, pulled back, pinned up, or falling straight down. Although people of color can achieve those styles, the requirements for them are antithetical to the expressive nature in the myriad cultures outside the walls of a corporation. In the African diaspora, as well as in native and indigenous communities, hair is sometimes used as an expression for a number of things, including tribal affiliations, marriage, and as an expression of individuality that stands out from the Eurocentric corporate environments; this can create a level of discomfort in the majority system which then labels these styles as unprofessional. Moreover, in modern times, having your hair in a color that stands out, like green, red, purple, or orange might also be deemed unprofessional and inappropriate.

Historically, corporate environments require uniformity. Think of the dark suit that so many of us have worn to an interview—there is indeed a uniform and an expectation of how one should dress in specific settings to be taken seriously. Conformity brings comfort, from appearance to speech. Don't get me wrong, I am fully aware that there are various ways to engage that are context specific; the way we talk to our friends and the language we may use in our homes may not align with day-to-day business expectations. If we again consider the notion of bringing your full self to work, it is something that I personally think is an impossible feat because bringing your full self, and being your full self, and expressing yourself in an unrestrained manner might not align with the company culture expectations or even the law. However, to create some opportunities for employees to bring more of themselves to work, many organizations have adopted a policy to ask an individual if they have a preferred name. Candidates or even employees might also be given the space to share their pronouns so that when conversations occur, they receive the respect that comes with an alignment on how they choose to show up in the world.

The question then becomes, is it realistic for organizations to expect employees to show up as their full selves and is it even a psychologically safe thing to request, knowing that the systems in which businesses operate are not sufficiently able to support when an individual can actually show up as their whole full self? In extreme cases, showing up one way can create hostility in others. I have often said that creating an inclusive environment requires a space safe enough that an individual can be themselves, but also not inhibit the right for someone else to do the same.

How do I cultivate a space where I am OK in my skin, feeling good about who I am, what I bring to the table, what I have going on? Business and governments have provided laws as guideposts, guardrails, and guidelines to help us cultivate an environment that is at a baseline for safety. For example, you might have an individual who feels comfortable looking at offensive material, such as pornography, at work. However, although it's legal to watch it in their private time, doing so at work can create a hostile environment, so, at a minimum, organizations should evaluate the principles outlined in workplace harassment to think about what else might be possible for some scaffolding on what it means to develop a psychologically safe workplace.

Benefits of Psychological Safety

Organizations undertake change initiatives for several reasons, including, but not limited to, legal compliance, economic conditions, a desire for innovation, edging out the competition for market share, social/community perception, and of course profitability. Placing a specific focus on psychological safety as an initiative is good for its own sake. However, there must be a business case to make it worthy of investment: "[Therefore] research has examined the relationship among psychological safety and outcomes such as innovation, creativity, employee attitudes, communication, knowledge-sharing, and voice behaviors" (Newman, Donohue, and Eva, 2017, p. 526). Findings indicate that psychological safety at individual and team levels reduces silence behaviors—in other words, people tend to speak up more, provide candid feedback, and point out errors to supervisors. These actions are critical to business performance since unspoken observations that could allow for improvements may be swept under the rug. Psychological safety also allows individuals to learn from failure, which is imperative for innovation, particularly risk taking (inclusive of social risk taking involved in extending trust) and experimentation. In fact, "there is growing evidence of a link between employee perceptions of psychological safety within the organization and their creativity" (Newman, Donohue, and Eva, 2017, p. 527). It would then make sense that a company would choose to focus on retaining the best and the brightest to continue supporting business outcomes. One additional benefit of psychological safety is a strong and positive link between it and employees' work attitudes such as organizational commitment (p. 527). As a business case for psychological safety, research indicates that "at high levels of psychological safety, the relationship between process innovativeness (i.e., the use of advanced manufacturing techniques) and profitability (i.e., return on assets), was positive, whereas at low levels of organizational psychological safety, the relationship was negative" (p. 528). According to the Center for Creative Leadership, people feel at ease bringing their complete, real selves to work and are willing to "put themselves on the line" in front of others when there is psychological safety in the workplace. Furthermore, businesses that foster psychologically secure work environments are better off because they allow staff members to voice concerns, ask bold questions, seek assistance, and take measured risks (Leading Effectively Staff, 2023).

Creating Psychological Safety

According to Timothy Clark (2020), there are four stages team members must move through for psychological safety to be established:

- Inclusion safety—feeling a sense of belonging and appreciation;

- Learner safety—freedom to ask questions, experiment, make and admit mistakes;
- Contributor safety—comfortable sharing ideas without fear of embarrassment; and
- Challenger safety—being able to question others, challenge ideas, or suggest changes to an approach.

Although I believe this is a great framework to think about how to practically focus on cultivating psychological safety, the reader should know that as of the writing of this chapter, the framework hasn't been empirically tested, so we can't say for sure that applying it will create more psychological safety.

Though psychological safety can be viewed as a shared responsibility, leaders have a significant role in its development. Research suggests the importance of managers engaging in supportive leadership behaviors, mainly "fostering bonds between team members, and leveraging supportive organizational practices" (Newman, Donohue, and Eva, 2017, p. 532). To give light to this, McKinsey's 2023 research found four qualities that can help mitigate tendencies of managers to exert control:

- *Awareness.* Acknowledge and accept that you have reactive tendencies and make time for self-reflection.
- *Vulnerability.* Model vulnerability during difficult times to help employees feel that they're not alone.
- *Empathy.* Demonstrate empathy to tap into what others are experiencing.
- *Compassion.* Compassion allows people to feel cared for and helps them pull through turbulent times.

The Center for Creative Leadership provides other considerations for leaders to cultivate psychological safety at work, including making psychological safety an explicit priority, facilitating space for everyone to speak up, establishing norms to handle failure, creating space for new ideas, embracing productive conflict, giving attention to patterns of who is experiencing more or less psychological safety, making an intentional effort to promote dialogue, and celebrating big wins.

To build psychological safety for today's high-performing teams, Baskin (2023) suggests creating space through day-to-day tasks for teams to bond to cultivate interpersonal ease. The more comfortable the team is together the greater the likelihood of transparency. Along the same vein as Timothy Clark's inclusion safety, Baskin suggests ensuring that all people feel "seen," and this can begin with simple inquiries about someone's overall well-being, or conversations that extend beyond the execution of the work itself.

Psychological Safety and Organization Culture Change

Creating a psychologically safe environment calls for deliberate attention to the nuanced experiences of everyone involved, and a desire to refine those experiences beyond transactional interactions and evolve to deeper human connections—ultimately, this is a culture change. Beyond profitability, organizations want to be around for the long haul, resilient, standing the test of time. "When leaders recognize the connections between psychological safety and resilience, they can model the behaviors that welcome candor—and set expectations throughout the organization to enhance integrity, innovation, and inclusion" (Gube and Hennelly, 2022). It is my view that the most resilient organizations have the ability to adapt. That said, according to Gube and Hennelly (2022), resilient organizations make time for psychological safety.

Here are the cultural dimensions they found critical for resilience:

- **Integrity:** "Organizations with a culture of integrity don't sacrifice doing the right thing for short-term profit." When employees feel safe, they demonstrate courageous candor and are less likely to take an external whistleblower approach with the government or the media.

- **Innovation:** Collaborative spaces that foster creativity without fear in sharing or retaliation for dissenting perspectives.

- **Inclusion:** Anchored in genuine respect and belonging. "Diverse teams have a broader knowledge base, which allows for better environmental scanning and risk analysis, especially in complex environments. Experiential diversity among team members increases the range of potential coping strategies and leads to better decision making under threat" (Gube and Hennelly, 2022).

Taking those three elements of resilience into consideration in the context of shifting the culture toward a psychologically safe environment, this work must be elevated as a strategic priority across all systems and processes in an organization and not relegated as an HR initiative. It should be planned out in the same ways that any large-scale organization-wide initiative would be (e.g., survey, focus groups, learning sessions, leadership updates on the importance of the shifts and how the business is doing), reconceptualizing the nature of the business with the understanding that this change will occur over time. That said, Gube and Hennelly share five focus areas for leaders in organizations to help make psychological safety a strategic priority in the service of organizational resilience:

1. **Ask questions about the culture.** Conduct assessments of engagement, integrity, and other aspects of culture from time to time. Monitor the results and define the existing and desired cultures with a clear plan on how to achieve the desired culture.

2. **Be clear about your expectations for ethical decision-making and integrity.** Create safe channels for sharing concerns and follow through on violations—and I'll add, especially for those in positions of power and influence.

3. **Encourage outside-the-box thinking.** "Reframe and celebrate mistakes as organizational learning opportunities. Assign and rotate the role of 'challenger' at meetings" (Gube and Hennelly, 2022).

4. **Invest in and personally support your DEI initiatives.** "Having even one ally in the workplace fosters a sense of belonging and can encourage people to speak up—be that ally. Use your privilege to share, rather than hoard, power. Foster diversity and inclusion as

explicit business strategies, include them in your ERG-related commitments, and tie them to executive compensation. Know how to avoid the pitfalls of disrespectful, non-inclusive cultures that make for toxic workplaces with high turnover. Prioritize clear communications, assign projects and roles based on strengths, foster relationships, and invite people to be part of the decision making" (Gube and Hennelly, 2022).

5 **Build accountability for psychological safety into performance metrics.** "Set relevant objectives and provide the necessary training for your managers so that psychological safety rises to the level of a strategic objective rather than a 'nice-to-have.' Emphasize leadership skills around emotional and social intelligence in career development and promotions. Take the metrics seriously and hold people accountable" (Gube and Hennelly, 2022).

In a research project presented to the faculty of the Graziadio Business School Pepperdine University by Sara Strueby (2019) for her M.Sc. in Organization Development, she shared what I would call the antithesis of what we've discussed about psychological safety playing out. A major finding from her study was that

> perceived psychological safety is impacted by perceptions of managers and the most prevalent theme displayed was manager favoritism towards individuals who share commonalities with the manager. Participants expressed that if they had a different opinion than that of their manager, they would not feel comfortable providing input (p. 21).

This particular finding highlights the impact and influence leaders have on creating a psychologically safe environment, mainly reward and punishment for alignment or divergence from his/her way of thinking. As previously discussed, psychologically safe environments embrace differences in opinion, which is important for innovation, and stop bad business decisions and bad actors before things are too far gone.

Other Considerations

There is some symbiosis between individual development and whole system integration needed for psychological safety. Individuals should embrace a growth mindset and lean into the sentiment that improvement can happen over time. Ironically, a growth mindset requires embracing failure and trying things that may come to someone else, skill-wise, very easily.

It's well understood that with any change efforts, resistance is inevitable. Feelings of frustration and anger are likely to come up, as well as other emotionally stressful responses. Leaders should anticipate and prepare for these responses, then monitor and address them as they come up during the change process. It might be helpful to understand the process of intentional behavior change from one of the most researched models on individual change, the Transtheoretical Model (TTM) of change created by James Prochaska and Carlo DiClemente (1983).

Through their integrated framework we gain insight into the five stages of progression and the strategies needed to guide someone through individual change:

- **Stage One: Precontemplation.** This is the time someone is lacking awareness of a need for change and therefore has no intention of changing.
- **Stage Two: Contemplation.** During this phase an individual has awareness that there is an issue and has started considering change without any committed action.
- **Stage Three: Preparation.** At this stage there is an intention to act soon, and the individual often starts making incremental steps to change.
- **Stage Four: Action.** This is the time when it is obvious that a commitment has been made to be immersed in making a change, indicated by time and energy dedicated to making things happen.
- **Stage Five: Maintenance.** At this stage, the change is considered stable due to the gains attained during the action stage.

With this understanding, the business can anticipate what kinds of emotions and behaviors may come up as employees are asked to embrace psychological safety. Better yet, leaders can proactively address some of the resistance, especially uninformed resistance which is "an unwillingness to consider the need for change because of lack of knowledge. It is a blind spot in the person's awareness; the person does not see what others see" (Hicks, 2014, p. 121).

Finally, Edmondson (2021) reminds us that when sharing the need for change, the way the work is framed is important. You'll want to focus on what's important and why you're embracing this change. Additionally, you'll want to remind people that the work being done is uncertain and has a lot of potential to go wrong. Making this statement creates an invitation to take the work seriously. Leaders will also want to model fallibility and invite input; by doing so, it helps others know that you need them to be part of the journey. You might say something like, "I may miss something, I need your help, so your input is crucial." Lastly, embrace messengers. Thank those who have the courage and willingness to offer their ideas and share their concerns. This will strengthen their willingness to do it again.

Creating and preserving psychological safety is not without its difficulties, even with its powerful advantages. Obstacles in the way can be caused by misplaced expectations, hierarchical organizations, and a fear of failing. Unexpected occurrences like business downturns or organizational reorganizations can also unintentionally jeopardize security. It is in these circumstances that adaptive leadership becomes critical. In order to uphold the fundamentals of psychological safety, leaders need to be transparent in their communication, show flexibility in modifying their approaches, and accept concerns. Organizations can successfully cross turbulent waters and guarantee that this essential component stays at the core of their company culture by accepting these problems and acting quickly to address them.

References

Associated Press (2023). Texas school again suspends Black student for refusing to change his hair. *Guardian*, www.theguardian.com/us-news/2023/dec/05/texas-black-student-suspended-hair-discrimination (archived at https://perma.cc/2GYN-UNEM)

Baskin, K. (2023). Four steps to building the psychological safety that high-performing teams need today. Harvard Business School, https://hbswk.hbs.edu/item/four-steps-to-build-the-psychological-safety-that-high-performing-teams-need-today (archived at https://perma.cc/YY73-9HSB)

Clark, T. (2020). *The 4 Stages of Psychological Safety (1st ed.).* Berrett-Koehler Publishers.

Edmondson, A. C. (1999). Psychological safety and learning behavior in work teams. *Administrative Science Quarterly*, **44**, 350–83.

Edmondson, A. C. (2002). The local and variegated nature of learning in organizations: A group-level perspective. *Organization Science*, **13** (2), 128–46.

Edmondson, A.C. (2021). Three ways to create psychological safety in healthcare, YouTube, www.youtube.com/watch?v=jbLjdFqrUNs (archived at https://perma.cc/6U9L-N4GT)

Gube, M. and Hennelly, D. S. (2022). Resilient organizations make psychological safety a strategic priority, *Harvard Business Review*, https://hbr.org/2022/08/resilient-organizations-make-psychological-safety-a-strategic-priority (archived at https://perma.cc/9JCP-EWG9)

Hicks, R. F. (2014). *Coaching as a Leadership Style.* Routledge.

Leading Effectively Staff (2023, January 10). What is psychological safety at work? How leaders can build psychologically safe workplaces, Center for Creative Leadership, www.ccl.org/articles/leading-effectively-articles/what-is-psychological-safety-at-work/ (archived at https://perma.cc/S2EC-XTKB)

McKinsey (2023). What is psychological safety? www.mckinsey.com/featured-insights/mckinsey-explainers/what-is-psychological-safety# (archived at https://perma.cc/WM5X-T6VZ)

Newman, A., Donohue, R., and Eva, N. (2017). Psychological safety: A systematic review of the literature. *Human Resource Management Review*, **27** (3), 521–35, www.sciencedirect.com/science/article/pii/S1053482217300013 (archived at https://perma.cc/S4TN-YKZ8)

Prochaska, J. O. and DiClemente, C. C. (1983) Stages and processes of self-change of smoking: toward an integrative model of change. *Journal of Consulting and Clinical Psychology*, **51** (3), 390–95

Spreitzer, G. M., Kizilos, M. A., and Nason, S. W. (1999). A dimensional analysis of the relationship between psychological empowerment and effectiveness, satisfaction, and strain. *Journal of Management*, **25** (3), 595–622.

Strueby, S. (2019) A research project presented to the faculty of the Graziadio Business School Pepperdine University by Sara Strueby for her Master of Science in Organization Development, https://digitalcommons.pepperdine.edu/cgi/viewcontent.cgi?article=2078&context=etd (archived at https://perma.cc/7E8T-Q2K4)

6

Supporting Employees as Catalysts

Merriam-Webster's dictionary defines a *catalyst* as "an agent that provokes or speeds significant change or action' (Merriam-Webster, n.d.). To consider employees as catalysts is to consider a shift in power dynamics from a top-down, formal, leadership-driven hierarchical perspective, to a bottom-up, critical mass point of view that acknowledges their impact and influence.

History has shown the power in mobilization and unification of people for a cause. In colonial India in 1930, Mohandas (Mahatma) Gandhi led what is known as the Salt March or Salt Satyagraha, one of the first acts of civil disobedience. Protests began from the fact that:

> Salt production and distribution in India had long been a lucrative monopoly of the British. Through a series of laws, the Indian populace was prohibited from producing or selling salt independently, and instead Indians were required to buy expensive, heavily taxed salt that often was imported. This affected the great majority of Indians, who were poor and could not afford to buy it (Pletcher, 2023).

The Salt March pushed British authorities to negotiate with leaders in India, which led to the British granting Indians access to the personal use of salt. Similarly, in the United States, influenced by the nonviolent approaches used by Gandhi, Dr. Martin Luther King Jr. was instrumental in organizing years of peaceful protests for Black Americans for equal rights, equal protection, and access to quality education. One of the events, known as the "Montgomery bus boycott, [was a] mass protest against the bus system of Montgomery,

Alabama, by civil rights activists and their supporters that led to a 1956 U.S. Supreme Court decision declaring that Montgomery's segregation laws on buses were unconstitutional" (Encyclopedia Britannica, n.d.). These and other notable events led to changes in legislation that had restricted Black Americans' access to previously segregated spaces.

Modern-day protests about police brutality, women's rights, anti-war evolvement, and the many international and domestic refugee crises have garnered media attention, placing pressure on those empowered with the ability to make change. You might be asking yourself, why political examples in a book on organization culture transformation? The answer is that they are the most salient representations of the impact and influence of galvanizing people within a political model of organizations. In other words, organizations are political in nature, and according to Aristotle, "man is a political animal." Marshak (2006) highlights:

> In both public and private organizations, the degree to which politics is, or should be, involved in organizational change seems to have two dominant perspectives. One is that organizations should be rational-logical instruments; the other that organizations, like all social collectives, are inherently political systems (p. 146).

In fact, "politics is the process of people using power to achieve their preferred outcomes" (p. 149). We're challenged to navigate the nuances of power—which is "the capacity to influence another person or group to accept one's own ideas or plans. In essence, power enables you to get others to do what you want them to do" (Greiner and Schien, 1988, p. 13). The locus of power can be downward (from leaders to subordinates), upward (from subordinates to leaders), or sideways (toward those that are neither leaders or subordinates) but is commonly concentrated downward. According to Godwin (2013), "There is no monopoly on power in our modern society, but a diverse 'power market' of sorts (imperfect and inefficient and irrational though it is) where individuals and institutions compete with one another for a share of power." Moreover, "To better work with the political dimension in organizational change, you need to be able to think about organizations as political as well as rational-logical systems" (Marshak, 2006, p. 151). It is my view that a deliberate shift in power dynamics that empowers employees to be catalysts and agents to drive change in organizations is the master key for transformation. This is certainly more easily said than done.

Influencing Influencers

One of the more practical ways to go about leveraging the power that exists within the employee base is by influencing the influencers. Ask yourself this question: Are you more or less inclined to trust a referral from someone you know or from a stranger? It can be said that "People prefer to say yes to individuals they know and like" (Cialdini, 2009, p. 172) and trust. "We are born with a propensity to trust... Through life experience, many of us have become less trusting— sometimes with good reason" (Covey and Merrill, 2006, p. 321). Recent history has associated influencers with social media, for example the likes of the Kardashians, Cristiano Ronaldo, Alex Hirschi, Huda Kattan, and Twitch streamer Kai Cenat, who was charged with inciting a riot in the summer of 2023 when thousands gathered in Union Square in New York City for a giveaway. In an article published by the United States Chamber of Commerce, Fallon, Medina, and Kubiak 2023 explain:

> Influencer marketing is about trust. By using an influencer for marketing campaigns, businesses benefit from having their brand vetted—by an influencer—before introducing a product or service to a potential customer base. If an influencer approves, consumers are more likely to trust the brand [...] Influencer marketing is social media marketing that leverages the influence of individuals with a dedicated social media following. Through the influencer, consumers engage with a business targeting them as potential customers.

Influencers have power to move people to act, behave, or even think in a particular way. That kind of power in the realm of social media is purchased, but in the world of work, the exchange is more nuanced with favoritism, preferential treatment, leeway, promotions, turning a blind eye, and other in-group behaviors. According to Ben-Ner et al. (2009):

> Generally, people act more favorably towards persons who share with them an important attribute of their identity compared to persons who differ significantly on that attribute... two studies suggest that attitudes and behaviors individuals exhibit towards others are affected strongly by the similarity of the identity of the two parties. Those that belong to the in-group are treated more favorably than those who belong to the out-group in nearly all identity categories and in all contexts.

For this type of in-group privilege, there needs to be some level of commonality, sameness, essentially moving in the same direction as others, all of which is antithetical to making change. The trick is identifying those with enough social capital and trust to position or support the desired change.

The work of Katz and Lazarsfeld on two-step flow of communication provides further insight (Katz, 1957). The prevalent paradigm in mass communication at the time was turned on its head by the hypothesis of the two-step flow of communication. Prior to Lazarsfeld's research, it was believed that a large audience that consumes and absorbs media messages is directly impacted by mass media. It was believed that media had a big impact on people's decisions and actions. However, studies by Lazarsfeld and colleagues revealed that, during a normal day, interpersonal conversations of political problems were more common than the intake of political news, and that only approximately 5 percent of people changed their preference for how they would vote as a result of media consumption.

Interpersonal interactions with friends, relatives, and people in one's social and professional circles have been shown to be more accurate indicators of a person's voting behavior than that person's media exposure (Postelnicu, 2016). Building on this foundation, Katz and Lazarsfeld gave the premise that "key people in a community set a trend which then provides a kind of 'all clear' signal for others, who then also adopt the change in attitude or behavior" (Steele, 1973, p. 131). Those giving the cues are influentials and determine what is permissible. If your organization can identify the influentials and obtain their buy-in, this could very likely be the fastest and most practical way of enabling employees as catalysts in driving organization change. For the organization development practitioner, this bottom-up approach is the best approach for lasting change and buy-in.

Understanding the Types of Change

When it comes to managing change, before embarking on the political challenge of influencing the influencers, it's important to keep in mind the various types of change that occur in organizations: structural, cost, process, and cultural (Encyclopedia of Management, 2019):

Structural change happens when there is a shift in the company's functional, divisional, or geographic configuration. A lot of companies experience these changes during a reorganization (reorgs), restructuring, acquisitions, or mergers. These kinds of shifts are often outcome-driven.

Cost changes happen when a company wants to reduce spending or expenses, often for greater efficiency and better performance. Organizations tend to achieve this through budget cuts, closing physical locations, reductions in force (RIFS), also known as layoffs, or redundancies, and the elimination of nonessential activities.

Process changes aim to improve the efficiency of organizational procedures not just in the development or creation of physical items but in collaborations and communication within and across teams, business units, and functions.

Cultural changes may be the most difficult to implement, as well as the most challenging to quantify. The Encyclopedia of Management (2019) states that "An organization's culture is its shared set of assumptions, values, and beliefs. A prototypical culture is the very bureaucratic, top-down style in which stability and standard processes are valued. When such an organization tries to adopt a more participative, involved style, this requires a shift in many organizational activities."

In addition to a shift in activities, there is also a need to redefine shared values, both implicit and explicit, as well as measures of accountability towards those values. Culture change also requires careful attention to change readiness:

> Companies must provide the right tools for people and make necessary improvements and adjustments in company systems and processes in order to tailor them to the planned changes. At the same time, they need to mitigate resistive factors. The continuous and integrated approach of change readiness requires the coordinated participation of everyone in the company, not just a few change agents or change leaders (Ferrara, 2013).

Some important questions to access readiness include:

- Is the desired change a real priority for us? Are we willing to put in the time and resources needed to make it happen?
- Given the current state of our business, operations, resources, and priorities, what can the organization as a whole realistically take on right now?
- What would we need to start, stop, or continue to make this change initiative a priority?
- What are the major blockers that would make this change impossible?
- If we made these changes, what measures of accountability are needed at all levels in the business to ensure that they know we are serious about the outcomes we desire to achieve?

> People react to changes with some kind of resistance because they do not understand how the changes will be implemented or how they will be affected by those changes... Employee resistance is not only a barrier to planned changes but also to innovative ideas... a high resistance to change will raise a question about the ability of management to

effectively implement change programs that require strong positive participation from company members. Instead of moving forward, the changes made at individual levels without support from company members may revert back to the status quo. Employees conduct a risk–return tradeoff of change management to analyze the expected returns of accepting changes, as well as the risks of doing so (Ferrara, 2013).

Communication

According to the Encyclopedia of Management (2019), management must take a number of measures to properly execute change, including important individuals, formulating a plan, supporting the plan, and communicating often. Most businesses struggle with the communication element. Decisions and plans are frequently made and implemented without enough consideration of the reasons behind the change, which can cause employees to become fearful, assume the worst, and become frustrated, all of which can breed resistance. It is essential to explain to staff members what is happening, why the changes are being made, and how they will progress. Increased communication can be utilized to comfort staff members and promote their continuous support, even if change can often cause a great deal of worry. Managers should be aware of any upward communication in addition to downward communication. They must be accessible to accept recommendations and respond to inquiries from staff. Change may be more successfully facilitated by providing opportunities for employee input, such as through meetings or an open-door policy for management.

Communication with Employees

It is nearly impossible for people to fully participate in the change process unless they are aware of the changes and how those changes will affect them. When a change project is starting, management should address any concerns raised by staff by providing them with pertinent information. They should also keep reiterating this information until the change is finished and assessed. This can be done by employing a variety of communication channels to let staff members know about changes, particularly ones that they can go over and review again. This will help individuals who are unable to attend in person, or who have neurodivergent learning styles, to absorb the information better. The message should detail the affected locations and the available support system for individuals affected, and should be straightforward and easy to grasp, based on common sense (Ferrara, 2013).

Employees as Catalysts for Change

According to Hill et al. (2012):

> Gaining employees' commitment is particularly important during radical change because it involves a fundamental, qualitative shift in the firm's philosophy or core perspective and strategic orientation [and furthermore] without the support of employees throughout the organization, radical change efforts are likely to fail (p. 758).

However, there is an important dynamic between the top management team and employees, since "radical organizational change is generally initiated by the top management team (TMT) and must then be implemented by employees at all levels of the organization" (p. 759). Research indicates that employees' reactions to change differ according to their hierarchical distance from the TMT. Therefore, it is very important that there are deliberate efforts to balance the advantages and disadvantages that come with that hierarchical distance, so providing employees across the company with an opportunity to be heard and engaged in a change process is imperative.

The Role and Significance of Employee Engagement

According to Cheung-Judge and Holbeche (2011):

> High-performance theory places employee engagement, or "the intellectual and emotional attachment that an employee has for his or

her work" (Heger, 2007) at the heart of performance, especially among knowledge workers. Of course every organization wants committed and enthusiastic people working for it and employee engagement is not a management fad (p. 63).

Shuck and Wollard (2010) define engagement as "an individual employee's cognitive, emotional, and behavioral state directed toward desired organizational outcomes" (p. 103). Many organizations invest in tools and resources to monitor employee engagement levels at least once a year. The tools and approaches used to gain insight into employee sentiment can be categorized under the umbrella term *listening systems*.

Getting the Pulse through Employee Listening Systems

One of the most popular listening tools is the survey. While many companies are good at gaining feedback from almost all levels of the business, most are not so great at reporting the findings. Surveys and questionnaires are great for organizational diagnosis; in other words they are helpful to identify the current state of a company. In an ideal world, the insights from these surveys should be shared systematically in phases, starting with the executive team, then deeper in the organization by level according to the formal hierarchy and within functional units or teams. Each team would have an opportunity to review their results, have a discussion, and begin considering plans for improvement. Leveraging employee perceptions as a grounding aspect of change and transformation can be pretty powerful, especially when there is an integrated symbiotic and deliberate effort to give feedback from the top down and from the bottom up.

Creating Safe Spaces to Process Challenging Experiences

In Chapter 5 we spent quite a bit of time exploring psychological safety, but before the term became a common part of the workplace lingua franca there was a lot of talk about creating safe spaces. In fact, "the term 'safe space' often gets thrown around, and mocked, in debates about social justice and free speech on college campuses. To some, safe spaces symbolize the 'coddling' of America's youth, the oversensitivity of modern progressivism, and even a serious threat to free speech" (Crockett, 2016). For a while the phrase was synonymous with higher education environments:

> On college campuses, a "safe space" is usually one of two things. Classrooms can be designated as academic safe spaces, meaning that students are encouraged to take risks and engage in intellectual discussions about topics that may feel uncomfortable. In this type of safe space, free speech is the goal. The term "safe space" is also used to describe groups on college campuses that seek to provide respect and emotional security, often for individuals from historically marginalized groups (Yee, 2019).

With the legacy of colonialism and the dominant cultures creating spaces that have been traditionally deemed the standard or norm, marginalized groups have had to adapt to those spaces. Let's be frank, not all safe spaces are created equal—spaces can never be completely safe:

> A safe space created by White people may not be safe for people of color. Being in a group of primarily White people may be a reminder of minorities' devalued status in society. Some Whites may need education about people of color. In contrast, people of color are constantly educated about White people. So, a safe space created by White people may mean additional work for people of color (Nagayama Hall, 2017).

Paul Axtell (2019), in his HBR article "Make Your Meetings a Safe Space for Honest Conversation," highlights that people have a desire to not only belong but to contribute and that teams can be provided that opportunity by applying two principles: giving permission and creating safety. We can completely express ourselves when we have permission to ask for what we want, offer feedback, and raise concerns when necessary. Ask yourself: What authorization from the group would you need to lead successfully? What authorization does the organization require from you to take part successfully? Second, individuals are more inclined to be open and honest during a meeting when they feel comfortable doing so. This will facilitate the expansion and depth of your interactions. In order to foster psychological safety in a meeting, it is recommended that the group give each speaker their undivided attention, give them time to finish their ideas, and share the insightful parts of each person's questions and comments.

The questions that emerge are: Who gets to speak? What ideas are worth sharing? and How can you cultivate a space that feels safe for everyone without anyone getting offended, feeling left out, or marginalized? Quite a tall order. The truth is, governments play a large part in laying the foundation of creating spaces that are free from experiences that can negatively impact employees and create a hostile work environment, a form of harassment. In the United States, harassment is a form of employment discrimination that violates Title VII of the Civil Rights Act of 1964, the Age Discrimination in Employment Act of 1967 (ADEA), and the Americans with Disabilities Act of 1990 (ADA) (U.S. Equal Employment Opportunity Commission, n.d.). According to the Society for Human Resource Management (SHRM, n.d.):

> A hostile work environment is created when harassing or discriminatory
> conduct is so severe and pervasive it interferes with an individual's
> ability to perform their job; creates an intimidating, offensive,
> threatening, or humiliating work environment; or causes a situation
> where a person's psychological well-being is adversely affected.

A psychologically safe environment has to be thoughtfully developed across multiple spaces and interactions. Kim and Del Prado (2019), in their book *It's Time to Talk (And Listen),* outline eight steps in the Kim Constructive Conversation Model, designed to create a space to discuss "personal experiences thoughts, feelings and beliefs on matters of culture and diversity, and to listen to the other person with genuine openness" (p. xiii), where healing is emphasized. Moreover:

> This means that the intention in having constructive conversations
> is not merely for external motives—to patch up an occasional
> misunderstanding or smooth out a few ruffled feathers in order to gain

others' approval or avoid future social faux pas. Rather, there is a clear and deliberate wish to be impacted deeply and purposefully—to be changed inside and out (p. xiv).

I don't know about you, but I'm not aware of many companies that are proactively aiming for that kind of change except when compelled to by scandal, lawsuit, or cancel culture. From my observation and experience their efforts are performative at best. But these constructive conversations, though pivotal, can be exhausting, and should be leveraged meaningfully, not everywhere or at all times, "since such conversations are not suited for all situations" (Kim and Del Prado, 2019, p. 11).

For those organizations truly interested creating deep roots across teams toward real culture transformation or change, consider applying the eight steps of the Kim Constructive Conversation Model. My advice is to leverage it from a personal, group, and organizational lens.

Town Halls

In 1633, Dorchester, Massachusetts, became the home of the nation's first town hall. According to the town's court records, residents met every Monday at 8 a.m. to adjudicate disputes and adopt "such orders as may contribute to the generally good as foresaid." The decisions taken during these sessions were regarded as binding on all men, "without gaynesaying or protest," and were respected as law. As a successful way for the populace to decide on significant concerns of the day, the practice quickly expanded throughout New England. Residents were able to voice their opinions on local matters through town hall meetings. The informal forum with majority rule formed the basis of early American democracy and continues to be employed across the nation (Mansky, 2016).

Town halls in a business setting often have senior leaders positioned to connect with employees and can be leveraged as an opportunity to share important information and insights. Some companies might refer to these gatherings as "all hands" meetings, and if done well they can create clarity and answer some of the most

TABLE 6.1 The Kim Constructive Conversation Model

Step	Name	Description
1	Identify a Goal	*Questions to get started:* • What is your goal in learning how to have constructive conversations about culture and diversity? • With whom, in what context, and regarding what topic would you most like to have constructive conversations? • What specific outcome are you seeking? *Possible goals:* • To stand up for a marginalized group • To stand up for myself • To share a different perspective • To genuinely understand where someone is coming from
2	Locate and Acknowledge Barriers	Understand blind spots within yourself and barriers that could get in the way and ask: *Is there anything about the identified goal that is challenging?* • Internal Barriers: The feelings, thoughts, and behaviors that could get in the way of goals: ○ Fear ○ Defensiveness ○ Fatigue • External Barriers: The factors outside of ourselves: ○ Social norms ○ Power and privileges
3	Setting a Value-Driven Intention	Values are the heart of this model, and this step, the most critical. By definition, values are those qualities and traits by which we measure our own and others' worth or merit (p. 47), and they guide our behavior. Determining values is a thoughtful process that shouldn't be rushed. *Consider the following questions:* • What character traits or behaviors matter to you? • What is the link between your values and goals? • What is the role your values might play in you actualizing your goals? • For each of the barriers listed in step two, identify a value that might help to mitigate it.

(continued)

TABLE 6.1 (Continued)

Step	Name	Description
4	Set the Stage	Open up the conversations with effective wording and delivery grounded in the core values: • Use "I" statements that are brief and concise • Choose words that reflect your openness and what you are about • Invite the listener to join you in a mutual engagement • Don't verbalize an opener that signals bad news • Consider timing, and ask: Is this a good time to do so? Am I in the right headspace to do this? What about audience readiness?
5	Take Action	Leverage the following three ingredients: • Why this person? Or why this particular audience? • My experience—thoughts, feelings, or concerns you want to share • The ask (why, me, ask)—what are you asking or seeking from the other person?
6	Listen	• Give your full undivided attention • Maintain eye contact • Turn your body toward and slightly lean to the other person • Check your face and body language • Offer an occasion uh-huh or a nod to convey you're tracking • Minimize distractions • Don't interrupt
7	Respond	Be thoughtful in a grounded values-based response that is not impulsive or reactive: • Acknowledge what was said • Share the impact • Hope for the future
8	Do it Again	Reflect on the steps that were taken and refine accordingly

pressing concerns employees have, especially when questions are gathered ahead of time.

These meetings are opportunities to connect with employees and take them out of their day, so your town halls should be well organized. It's best practice to share the meeting focus and resources to capture questions. Some companies choose to partner with their communications department to help facilitate questions to the leaders and to filter questions that were submitted before the meeting or those that come in real time: "It also is critical for each business function, including finance, HR, sales and engineering, to provide updates about where they stand and what they are planning" (Ora Lobell, 2022).

To improve the town hall experience, consider keeping the meetings short and making the agenda fresh and nonrepetitive in terms of content shared in other similar forums. Although the business might find this to be a great opportunity to reiterate certain messages, it can be frustrating from an employee perspective to hear content that has already been shared in other contexts, making a particular town hall meeting feel redundant.

I have attended town hall meetings that were positioned more like podcast interviews between leaders and some other team member. One of the best opportunities to leverage that kind of a setting is when a new leader joins an organization, particularly when there may be some trepidation about the scope of the work that this individual would be leading, or maybe the reputation of the company this person is coming from. In those particular meetings, there were moments of candor, where a leader had an opportunity to share their vision and their values to create a baseline around what the business or division might expect in terms of the way forward. There are also moments set aside for Q&As, with questions coming directly from the crowd or from online. When done well, this creates an opportunity for employees in the organization to get an initial glimpse of the leader's perspective and style of communication, and bridge the gap between answered questions.

In my own career, there have been some missed opportunities to leverage town hall meetings to formally introduce myself to the company and facilitate the space for me to share the vision that I held for the work I was shepherding. In my view, the barriers to leveraging an all-hands or town hall meeting with me stemmed from what I believe were the organization's attempt to pause progression of initiatives and/or control the narratives around some of the changes that were coming and who would be the face of those changes. Given those dynamics, what I did instead was schedule meetings with senior leaders and stakeholders across the organization to share a high-level vision of the work. Although formal alignment of that vision took quite some time, the process of alignment was an indicator of what the business valued at a particular point in time.

Office Hours

Sometimes companies set aside time within a department to allow for questions or to share resources with employees, and refer to this time as formal office hours. I've leveraged this concept during specific times that were challenging for employees. One example of this took place after a business had experienced layoffs. I set aside office hours, which was a block of time on a specific day, where I made myself available to support individuals who were having a difficult time processing the layoffs that had just occurred. I limited access to this particular "office hours" experience to leaders of the various employee resource groups (ERGs).

The way I structured the office hours was by creating a Zoom meeting that was shared on a specific online platform with a message around the duration that I would be available and what I hoped would be a space for employees to connect with me and with each other. My approach was more of creating a drop-in experience where people could hop on and hop off the call. The experience was very well received. I would encourage leaders to create office hours across the company after a town hall meeting, to create a more intimate space to connect with employees who may have otherwise been less inclined to engage in a larger all-hands forum.

One-on-Ones

If you've ever scheduled a meeting with another colleague, team member, or your direct manager, you've had a one-on-one that facilitates the ability to connect on a more personal level. These meetings can be as short as five minutes or as long as a couple of hours, depending on the purpose of the call. For example, you might meet with your manager to share details on the progress of a project, or connect with a colleague to get to know them better on a human level, without ever mentioning the work. You can also connect with a stakeholder to get their help and guidance on how to move past challenges and barriers you might be facing and share resources that might be mutually beneficial.

There have been moments where I have leveraged one-on-ones, even while holding a senior leadership position, with individuals deeper in the organization. The moments I chose to do so were high-stakes issues that fell under the work that I had direct responsibility for. I extended the invitation to the individual who raised the concern to meet with me. There were multiple reasons I did so, including getting an opportunity to understand their perspective and giving them a chance to feel heard by someone in a senior leadership position. I didn't do this frequently—only at moments where I felt it was important to quell what could become an explosive situation.

In a similar vein, it may be useful to leverage influential individuals within the organization to have strategic opportunities to connect with employees on a one-on-one basis. This might be having influencers meet with other influencers, providing an opportunity to share strategy on how to help to shift the business's direction, particularly around the most troublesome challenges and barriers that might stand in way of implementing a particular shift that the business is trying to achieve.

Irrespective of the modality chosen, whether in large groups such as a town hall, during office hours with smaller groups, or even a one-on-one meeting, we need to keep in mind that these are all significant touch points to connect with employees to learn how to both convey a desired change and to learn of the commitments and barriers employees have toward embracing a given change.

References

Axtell, P. (2019). Make your meetings a safe space for honest conversation, *Harvard Business Review*, https://hbr.org/2019/04/make-your-meetings-a-safe-space-for-honest-conversation (archived at https://perma.cc/M5SL-RMXP)

Ben-Ner, A., McCall, B. P., Stephane, M., and Wang, H. (2009). Identity and in-group/out-group differentiation in work and giving behaviors: Experimental evidence. *Journal of Economic Behavior & Organization*, **72** (1), 153–70.

Cheung-Judge, M-Y and Holbeche, L. (2011) *Organization Development* (p. 363) Kogan Page, Kindle Edition.

Cialdini, R. B. (2009). *Influence: Science and Practice* (Vol. 4). Boston, MA: Pearson Education.

Covey, S. M. and Merrill, R. R. (2006). *The Speed of Trust: The One Thing That Changes Everything*. Simon and Schuster.

Crockett, E. (2016). Safe spaces, explained. Vox, www.vox.com/ 2016/7/5/11949258/safe-spaces-explained (archived at https://perma.cc/ UG5K-ESZ6)

Encyclopedia Britannica (n.d.) Montgomery bus boycott, www.britannica.com/ event/Montgomery-bus-boycott (archived at https://perma.cc/44TV-F7JW)

Encyclopedia of Management (2019) *Managing Change*, 8th ed., Vol. 2, pp. 705–08. Gale. Retrieved from www.gale.com/ebooks/9781410389350/ encyclopedia-of-management (archived at https://perma.cc/U8EX-DJTF)

Fallon , N., Medina, J., and Kubiak, L. (2023) Get connected: Top 5 social media influencers in 9 industries. US Chamber of Commerce, www.uschamber.com/co/ grow/marketing/top-social-media-influencers (archived at https://perma.cc/ 8M7F-F8HT)

Ferrara, M. H. (Ed) (2013) Guiding employees through change. In M. H. Ferrara (Ed.) *Gale Business Insights Handbook of Cultural Transformation* (pp. 229–237). Gale, https://link-gale-com.proxy.library.nyu.edu/apps/doc/ CX2759200029/GVRL?u=new64731&sid=bookmark-GVRL&xid=010f2aba (archived at https://perma.cc/5LSG-2GW6)

Godwin, J. (2013). *The Office Politics Handbook: Winning the Game of Power and Politics at Work*. Career Press.

Greiner, L. E. and Schien, V. E. (1988). *Power and Organization Development: Mobilizing Power to Implement Change*. Addison Wesley.

Hill, N. S., Seo, M. G., Kang, J. H., and Taylor, M. S. (2012). Building employee commitment to change across organizational levels: The influence of hierarchical distance and direct managers' transformational leadership. *Organization Science*, **23** (3), 758–77.

Katz, E. (1957). The two-step flow of communication: An up-to-date report on an hypothesis. *Public Opinion Quarterly*, **21**, 61–78. https://doi.org/ 10.1086/266687 (archived at https://perma.cc/V2E5-4MJZ)

Kim, A. S. and Del Prado, A. (2019). *It's Time to Talk (and Listen): How to Have Constructive Conversations about Race, Class, Sexuality, Ability & Gender in a Polarized World*. New Harbinger Publications.

Mansky, J. (2016). The history of the town hall debate, Smithsonian, www. smithsonianmag.com/history/history-town-hall-debate-180960705/ (archived at https://perma.cc/E5WZ-RE5R)

Marshak R. (2006). *Covert Processes at Work: Managing the Five Hidden Dimensions of Organizational Change.* Berrett-Koehler

Merriam-Webster. (n.d.). Catalyst. www.merriam-webster.com/dictionary/catalyst (archived at https://perma.cc/D5HY-D8H2)

Nagayama Hall, G. C. (2017). Creating safe spaces: Safety for one group may not be safety for another. *Psychology Today*, www.psychologytoday.com/us/blog/ life-in-the-intersection/201707/creating-safe-spaces (archived at https://perma. cc/9UAU-68LM)

Ora Lobell, K. (2022) How to run employee town hall meetings post pandemic. SHRM, www.shrm.org/resourcesandtools/hr-topics/employee-relations/pages/ how-to-run-employee-town-hall-meetings-post-pandemic.aspx (archived at https://perma.cc/XR29-LWQ3)

Pletcher, K. (2023). Salt March. *Encyclopedia Britannica*, www.britannica.com/ event/Salt-March (archived at https://perma.cc/A6KL-WAYS)

Postelnicu, M. (2016). Two-step flow model of communication. *Encyclopedia Britannica*, www.britannica.com/topic/two-step-flow-model-of-communication (archived at https://perma.cc/E7M9-4XPH)

Shuck, B. and Wollard, K. (2010). Employee engagement and HRD: A seminal review of the foundations. *Human Resource Development Review*, **9**, 89–110

SHRM (n.d.) HR Glossary, www.shrm.org/topics-tools/tools/hr-glossary#H (archived at https://perma.cc/R3QL-KQBR)

Steele, F. I. (1973). *Physical Settings and Organization Development.* Addison-Wesley.

U.S. Equal Employment Opportunity Commission (n.d.). Harassment. www.eeoc. gov/harassment (archived at https://perma.cc/J67D-U7ES)

Yee, M. (2019) Why "safe spaces" are important for mental health—especially on college campuses. Healthline, www.healthline.com/health/mental-health/ safe-spaces-college# (archived at https://perma.cc/8UH2-P368)

7

Partnerships Needed for Achieving Culture Transformation

Change work is not a solo endeavor. In fact, there aren't many changes that happen in business without some level of collaboration, buy-in, or sign-off from another group or person. In the consulting world, stakeholder engagement is a foundational piece of a change management process, and by stakeholders I'm referring to an individual, group, department, or entity that would be impacted directly or indirectly by the proposed change. With a definition like that you'd be inclined to think that everyone is a stakeholder, and you wouldn't be wrong. The reality is that there are different levels of engagement and involvement of stakeholders in general and at various points in the change process.

For those of you in the project management world, the RACI chart is foundational when identifying stakeholders. RACI stands for Responsible, Accountable, Consulted, and Informed. These categories help to sift through the broad range of stakeholders in an organization and create a level of prioritization needed to ensure the right people receive the right information at the right time. This isn't a process that happens in a vacuum; it requires talking with numerous people over time to weigh in and refine the list in a sort of snowball effect that, once complete, will serve as your go-to resource of whom to go to for what.

While the RACI chart is a helpful tool, it doesn't provide guidance on how to build partnerships in organizations. When it comes to culture change, the principles and practices in the field of organization development (OD) are the gold standard. "Organization development is a planned process of change in an organization's culture through the utilization of behavioral science technologies, research, and theory" (Burke and Noumair, 2015, p.12). OD is also a collaborative and inclusive process that advocates for involving people in decisions that directly affect them (Carasco, 2021). When you involve people in the process of change you have a better chance of that change enduring.

Organization development models for change in organizations typically involve a systematic approach in order to enhance effectiveness. They often begin with assessing the current state, identifying areas for improvement, and involving employees in the change process. Implementation includes communication, training, and continuous evaluation to ensure sustainable growth. Successful models foster a collaborative culture, emphasizing flexibility and responsiveness to evolving challenges. The OD model for change happens in phases:

> Each phase has particular aspects to give attention to, including but not limited to, exploring the match/comfort with the client, evaluating the client's readiness for change, understanding the resources available to do the work, client expectations, ground rules for communication, determining data analysis, evaluation, and feedback, action planning, conflict resolution, determining success, and ending the client engagement (Carasco, 2021).

When it comes to culture transformation, it's important to ground expectations in a journey-based mindset. While some changes can happen quickly, others may happen in waves over time. The factors that determine the speed of change include leadership support, employee buy-in, business constraints, resource allocation, and overall commitment. The next section will cover stakeholder identification using OD methodologies as a foundation for partnerships.

Stakeholder Identification

A project cannot be established and accomplished—and the project benefits realized—without carefully considering and dealing with the project stakeholders... [Moreover] project stakeholder management thus consists of two types of activities: conducting project stakeholder analyses to provide the information needed for stakeholder management and, on the basis of the results of these analyses, interacting purposefully with the project stakeholders (Eskerod and Jepsen, 2013, p. 7).

At a high level, stakeholder identification begins with questions around who will be impacted by the project and its deliverables, how they will contribute to its success, and who should receive priority. Stakeholder identification goes beyond making a list; it's a thoughtful and thorough process that considers ways of engaging with and leveraging expertise inclusively.

There's nothing worse than feeling left out when you should be pulled in. I've been on both sides. That's why it's critical to have an iterative process that begins with a project stakeholder assessment to generate and validate those who should be involved. Eskerod and Jepsen (2013) note that a stakeholder assessment will allow you to:

- Clarify the contributions needed (if any) from each stakeholder;
- Get an understanding of each stakeholder in terms of the benefits that the stakeholder will value in terms of project outcomes as well as concerns regarding potential drawbacks and costs;
- Give insights into each stakeholder's potential to "harm" and "help" the project.

From your robust list of stakeholders, you can now determine the partners that it would be helpful for you to work more closely with for the long-term goal of culture transformation. As with any relationship, you'll need to put in some deliberate time to cultivate a trust-based relationship, which might require you to spend time with your colleagues in formal settings at the office by way of meetings, team calls, and in-office social events as well as informal settings such as happy hours, team lunches, or coffee breaks. For the introverted leaders reading this section, I can imagine your anxiety level may have risen just a touch higher, but let me assure you that relationship building isn't one size fits all. Don't betray yourself for yourself. Instead, choose to connect with your colleagues in ways that are true and reasonable for you and honor your needs and preferences. Keep in mind that the best relationships are mutually beneficial. You'll want to consider what would be helpful to your future partners and how you can support them as well. The best way to find out is to ask. Ask those who know them and understand their interests, and ask them directly.

Keep in mind that partnerships in the social impact sector are at a turning point when success demands a new way of thinking. Despite the abundance of new models, impact can still be difficult to attain even with the unprecedented quantity and variety of relationships. A few of the strategies that make partnership work attractive are corporations collaborating with NGOs, purpose brands, public-private partnerships, cross-sector collaborations, the emergence of shared value, strategic alliances, and branded cause partnerships. However, it is also becoming more difficult to cut through the noise and establish meaningful partnerships (Georgetown, 2023).

Partnerships Needed by Levels in the Organization

Executive Leaders

It's important to have the support of executive leaders in your organization to move change initiatives forward. These are the most senior people who tend to report to the head of the company. In an ideal world all the leaders would get behind the work you're leading, and you wouldn't have many hurdles. In fact, I've had moments with executive leaders who were all in, visibly present, vocal, and supportive during a change process. I have also experienced what it is like to be ignored, pushed out, and have the work deprioritized. One thing you don't want is to have a leader publicly put down a project that you're driving, but just know that it happens. Do you need the support of an entire executive team? Or could one or two allies be enough? It depends. I will say that your best bet is to identify one or two executive leaders who are supportive of the change initiative and to spend time cultivating those relationships so that you have enough rapport with them to convince them to spend some of their "social capital" with their peers on the leadership team in support of your efforts. You'll want to identify someone who has a high level of integrity and a voice with impact influence. Be careful not to go for the most vocal or extroverted person; take time to evaluate their character, reputation, and the initiatives they support. Having one or two allies with the right levels of commitment can make all the difference in bringing attention and importance to your work when you're not in the room.

Senior Leaders

Senior leaders would be the next layer down from the executive team. These leaders manage leaders, and as you may have surmised, the impact and influence of leaders on leaders is paramount. They are critical players in the proverbial cascading of messaging from the top down, needed to communicate the importance of an initiative deeper and more broadly across the company. In the most formal sense, the messages can be pre-scripted from your communications team and shared in a written or verbal format during leadership team meetings or via team mailing lists, comms channels, etc. The more powerful impact, however, comes from those informal meetings, off-sites, or "water cooler" conversations where folks are looking for less formal reflections on the changes happening in the company.

Middle Managers

Jaser (2021) said it best when she noted that middle managers "are the engine of the business, the cogs that make things work, the glue that keeps companies together." Gilbert (2009) highlighted that historically, middle-level managers served as the crucial bridge linking a small group of top executives in an organization to the extensive workforce responsible for the majority of its productivity. The role was fairly transactional, with middle managers receiving strategic instructions from executives that were then translated into detailed actions, shared with individual contributors. This structured flow from strategy to tactic to execution allowed the company to maintain operations at a deliberate pace. Gilbert goes on to say:

> In the fundamental role as a leader of change, middle managers—the mid-level leaders—need to help everyone around them change the way they perceive and approach change, from an extrinsic (compelled) to an intrinsic (desired) viewpoint. In order to support this fundamental role, four role imperatives emerge as "agent provocateur."

This can be accomplished by: a) creating an adoption mindset—what it takes to adopt the change; b) creating an ownership and accountability mindset up and down the organization—who owns the change; c) realizing the benefits—as a result of the change, what benefits will be realized; and d) securing the ROI.

Chiefs of Staff

The Chief of Staff (CoS) role has become more common in recent years. This role has traditionally been linked to military and political settings but has been adopted by startup companies in recent years to offer extra support to their leadership teams. From my experience, the CoS position supports a senior leader in a given business unit as a lead program manager, driving various business operations, operationalizing initiatives, and helping to organize and stitch things together across an organization. More broadly:

> Within a company or organization, a chief of staff is an executive-level employee who supports the chief executive officer (CEO), chief operating officer (COO), and other top-level executives. A chief of staff typically supervises and communicates with lower-level staff members, providing project management, and implementing strategic planning processes (MasterClass, 2022).

I've experienced both helpful and obstructive individuals sitting in this seat. It's helpful to understand their motivations, ways of working, and how supporting or participating in your change work would help them, which I suppose applies to all stakeholder groups.

When well positioned, a CoS can be an exceptional communication liaison between executive team members and other staff including department heads. They are also strong in the area of consultation, providing data analysis and metrics of the company's productivity to the executive team and overall team performance. A CoS can help you to prioritize tasks since they often play a role supporting the schedules of executive team members. Well beyond the administration aspects of the work, a good CoS can support your change initiative as a problem-solving partner. They can help to identify challenges and provide workable solutions. Finally, a CoS is great at project assessment and facilitation, and can help to evaluate the risk, cost, and effort involved in achieving the goal, then guide and supervise the enterprise to its successful completion.

Executive Assistants

Formally known as secretaries, executive assistants are also important partners in change initiatives. They are the gatekeepers of the calendars of many of the individuals that you will be trying to book time with, and so it's important to learn from them what challenges the leaders are facing and to gain insight and understanding on when is the best time to connect with a leader about a specific topic.

Individual Contributors

If you are able to galvanize individuals within an organization around a single priority, you will do well in seeing a change initiative move forward. Individual contributors are those who do not have anyone reporting to them, but are focused on the scope of work that is within their skill set to help to drive business results. They are the foot soldiers within the organization and are exceptionally important in sustaining the change.

Employee Resource Groups

Employee resource groups are organizations that facilitate a space for individuals to connect based on a number of criteria, which may or may not include gender, race, sexual identity, ethnicity, veteran status, and even parental status. However, when it comes to partnerships needed for driving change and organization, leveraging employee resource groups as strategic partners in messaging the importance of a specific direction could help to galvanize and enroll individual contributors across the organization.

The Marginalized

Finally, you want to consider how you might involve and engage those who may feel marginalized within your organization. Sometimes individuals who may feel marginalized tend to have viewpoints that do not align with the majority voices on a specific topic or business direction. They may very well be called the naysayers in the organization. Don't underestimate their influence or ability to disrupt what it is that you're trying to drive across the company; from a change management standpoint these individuals can be classified as potential blockers, so it's important to understand their viewpoints, and consider ways in which you might obtain their buy-in and support. If it's not possible to gain their support, we have to consider ways to mitigate their impact and influence on driving the change forward.

Partnerships Needed by Business Unit

After you've had an opportunity to clarify organization-level partnerships, you'll want to create a new list of partners by function, which is likely to overlap with the organization-level partnerships. For the sake of brevity, the functional partnerships I'd encourage you to explore are in the revenue engine of the organization, human resources, the social collectives (employee experiences), and the most influential people in the organization with formal and informal power and authority.

The Revenue Engine

Without the sales team there wouldn't be an organization at all. They are the revenue-generating engine of the company and put a significant amount of time and energy into building relationships. Typically, the sales team operates independently, although they can form teams focused on specific regions or products within their organization. For instance, they might sell fast-moving consumer goods (FMCGs) like clothing or pharmaceuticals to high-street chain buyers, offer IT solutions to blue-chip businesses, or market cars to fleet buyers in major multinationals. Working toward sales goals, these professionals are motivated and incentivized, dedicating a significant portion of their time to interacting with buyers and customers rather than spending extensive time at the central office with the rest of the team (Vinturella and Erickson, 2013). Partnering with the sales organization will allow you to understand where the business is in terms of overall financial health. Sales are captured in earnings statements which also offer a synopsis of income and expenditures. With this clarity you'll have a good sense of where the business will focus attention and resources, an invaluable insight as to the viability of the work you want to move forward in terms of where people are focused and if your work will garner the attention and commitment needed.

Human Resources

According to Carasco and Rothwell (2020), human resources (HR) encompasses two dimensions:

1 The tangible workforce, comprising individuals employed within the company.

2 A strategic entity within the organization responsible for overseeing people operations to facilitate successful business results. This entails:

  o Managing benefits and compensation administration;

  o Facilitating recruitment, onboarding, performance management, and training;

- Formulating strategies for retention, workforce planning, diversity and inclusion, risk management, employee relations, and change management.

In most organizations the HR team has business partners within their function that work and collaborate with leaders in various parts of the company. They have a pulse on the challenges and concerns faced by leaders, managers, and employees and can also be very helpful in supporting messaging change management at all stages of the integration process.

The Social Collectives

The social collectives represent the variety of employee experience options available in an organization. They include things like participation in an employee resource group (ERG), social impact initiatives, a sports team, town hall meetings, or even things like company-sponsored happy hours, etc. There are several benefits to participating in social activities at the workplace, including but not limited to fostering employee well-being. Smith and Johnson (2018) published a study on social interactions at work and found that the interactions are linked to increased satisfaction and overall job performance. Brown and Williams (2019) found that participating in social activities builds camaraderie with team members, which improves collaboration. Some of you may have already experienced the stress relief that can come from engaging in social interactions. A study by Garcia and Martinez (2020) highlights that employees who are part of regular social activities experience improved mental health; moreover, socializing at work provides an avenue for people to support each other through shared experiences, which can lead to more connection and resilience (Jones et al., 2017). Social events tend to positively influence employee engagement.

Thompson and Davis (2016) highlight that employees who are actively involved in workplace social activities tend to be more engaged and committed to their roles, which translates into increased productivity and a stronger sense of belonging. If your partnership with the social collective can garner a level of engagement to support your change initiative, it's worth understanding what keeps employees engaged, particularly as it relates to company culture. In fact, when employees have social interactions, it cultivates shared values, which are foundational components of a healthy organizational culture (Roberts and Anderson, 2018). All of this can contribute to increased employee retention rates and a more desirable position choice-wise in the global talent marketplace for potential recruits (Lee and Kim, 2019). The benefits of participating in social activities at work are well documented, and these activities contribute to enhanced job satisfaction, reduced stress, increased engagement, and the development of a positive organizational culture. Encouraging social interactions in the workplace is a valuable investment in fostering a cohesive and productive workforce. You need to think about how to meaningfully engage within these social collectives. Connecting with the teams that organize or sponsor these events will provide you with access to channels to engage with various stakeholder groups across the company at different stages of the change process.

The Most Influential

In some organizations there are people who seem to have a significant amount of influence on the behaviors of others. You'll want to find them and share what you're looking to accomplish. I spent some time in another chapter on influencing the influencers; however, based on the categories that we have discussed so far in this chapter, you'll want to gain an understanding of who within the business has direct or indirect influence, and how they influence in terms of the mechanisms, whether it be use of internal blogs or posting Slack messages, or having impromptu meetings to discuss things. Dig into how they leverage whatever tools are available within the organization to convey their point of view and consider ways you can partner with them, first by strategizing how you might be able to share and leverage their participation in the change initiative, using the same mechanisms.

Examples of Internal Partnerships

"To date, no single consistent definition of social impact has been developed in the literature. This is in part due to social impact being discussed from different perspectives in different disciplines, including psychology, sociology and management" (Brzustewicz et al., 2022). The impact an organization has on society is often referred to in management literature as the outcomes, effects, or repercussions that the organization's activities (such as projects or operations) have on individuals and the overall development of society. This impact can range from physical and emotional aspects of individuals' lives to areas such as health, education, working conditions, and overall well-being. They can also extend from individual impacts to community-wide effects. The social impact of an organization can be observed in areas like employment and the labor market, the quality of jobs, social inclusion and the protection of vulnerable groups, gender equality, the impact on individuals' private and family lives, public health and safety, access to and the effects of social protection, health, and education systems, as well as culture.

Brzustewicz et al. (2022) highlight a case of social impact initiated by a group of employees who have family members with autism. The connection to and momentum for the work began with extensive internal communication around volunteering that received positive responses from supervisors:

> The incorporation of the employees' initiative into the [corporate volunteering] program enhanced their motivation to get involved in the project, and thus allowed them to continue a long-term tradition of company engagement in creating something good for society. The company–NGO contacts at the pre-[corporate volunteering] stage helped both parties get to know each other's expectations and the specificity of their functioning, leading to an agreement on common goals, as well as on resources and activities needing to be allocated in the collaboration (Brzustewicz et al. 2022).

The following are some examples of social impact partnerships that leverage employee participation.

IBM's Corporate Service Corps: IBM created the Corporate Service Corps, a global pro bono consulting program that gives their employees an opportunity to collaborate with local organizations in service to addressing challenges in society. A fabulous way to allow employees to meaningfully tap into their day jobs (IBM, 2023)

Salesforce 1-1-1 Model: Salesforce began their 1-1-1 model, which commits 1 percent of their equity, 1 percent of their product, and 1 percent of employee time to philanthropic efforts. This encourages employees to actively participate in various social impact initiatives and is becoming a type of model for other companies to follow (Salesforce, 2023)

Google's Google.org Impact Challenge: One of the ways Google engages employees is via its philanthropic efforts at the Google.org Impact Challenge. Sometimes employees might struggle to see how their day jobs can make a difference, and this is another great example of employees contributing their day-to-day expertise to support the organization's global issues (Google, 2023).

Unilever's Sustainable Living Plan: Unilever's Sustainable Living Plan encourages employees to participate in achieving sustainability goals. The company asks the workforce to contribute ideas and solutions for reducing environmental impact and improving social conditions (Unilever, 2023).

External Partnerships to Consider

We've spent some time outlining the internal partnerships needed for a successful organization culture transformation inclusive of employees and leadership at various levels in the company. I'd like to propose some partnerships outside of your organization that can yield several benefits grounded in expanding both perspective and expertise. External partnerships can be expanded to customers, thereby helping you to anchor the impacts of change initiatives in an understanding of customer expectations. Equally important are potential partnerships with regulators, which can be crucial for a successful and sustainable transformation, especially when there may be some disruption to ways of working. Another external partnership to consider is partnership with external consultants who are subject matter experts in certain lines of business or technical areas, or with experts in organization change, culture, and strategy. Finally, you should consider partnering with industry peers. These collaborations can offer great opportunities for benchmarking and shared learning experiences. Moreover, opening up collaboration with external partners, inclusive of competitors, can bring diverse skills and expertise that may complement and enhance your organization's capabilities in areas like innovation and cost efficiency, and might even aid in establishing a market foothold or opening doors to new business opportunities. The following are examples in each of these areas.

Partnership That Led to Innovation

Meta and EssilorLuxottica: Meta partnered with the world's largest eyewear company, EssilorLuxottica, to co-create and sell smart glasses under the brand Ray-Ban. This partnership combined expertise in tech with experience in eyewear to create a new product for a broader market, an example of leaning into a company's individual strength to make something new (Meta, 2023).

Partnership That Provided Cost Efficiency

Ford and General Motors: Two of the largest automakers in the world partnered to develop the next generation of fuel-efficient engines. This partnership allowed both companies to bring new fuel-efficient vehicles to the market more quickly while sharing the costs of innovation and experimentation (Healey and Woodyard, 2013)

Partnerships That Created New Business Ventures

Starbucks and Kraft Foods: Starbucks and Kraft Foods partnered to launch a line of ready-to-drink Starbucks coffee beverages. This partnership expanded Starbucks' reach into new markets, while granting Kraft Foods access to Starbucks' brand recognition and marketing expertise (Baertlein, 2011).

Partnerships That Created a Market Foothold

Tesla and Panasonic: Tesla partnered with Panasonic, a major electronics company, to co-develop and produce lithium-ion batteries for Tesla's cars. This partnership allowed Tesla to simultaneously reduce costs while scaling up its battery production. Panasonic benefited by cornering the market in the expanding electric vehicle industry (Panasonic, 2023).

Apple and Intel: Apple and Intel, a semiconductor manufacturer, partnered to develop processors for Apple computers. The partnership gave Apple access to the latest processor technology, and it helped Intel to maintain its market share as a leading supplier of processors (Leswing, 2020).

In summary, external collaborations contribute to organizational growth, resilience, and the ability to navigate an ever-evolving business landscape. Partnerships can develop into strategic alliances, offer learning opportunities, new business ventures, expand global reach, accelerate product development, and even provide some risk mitigation. By building strong partnerships with these stakeholders, a company can navigate the complexities of organizational transformation more effectively.

Partnership with Yourself

Finally, there is no greater partnership than the one you make with yourself. It might sound a bit strange, but every relationship we have hinges on the value of and the agreements we hold about ourselves. I want to challenge you to pause and consider what I am putting forward. It might make a bit more sense when anchored in a negotiation perspective. If you've ever gone shopping in an area where haggling is the norm, or you made a big purchase of a property or a vehicle, or even asked for a higher salary than what was initially offered to you, you'll understand that being prepared with a decision on what you are willing to pay and what you're not willing to pay is a key starting point for any "buyer" in a negotiation. There is clarity in your position based on things like what you can afford, and sometimes even the likelihood of finding the thing you want again. In a similar manner, establishing partnerships requires a comparable level of personal anchors. You should have clarity on things like:

- The kind of partnerships you need;
- The ways you communicate and how much flexibility you have in you to shift for others;
- What would end a partnership or are dealbreakers.

All of these considerations are anchored in self-awareness and relationship management: knowing how you influence others and how they impact you, while acting in congruence with your values and limitations.

You are responsible for your own health. You are responsible for your own well-being. Remember that the business is going to prioritize the business, and you're going to need to prioritize yourself. So, what does taking care of yourself look like? Although it can vary from individual to individual, there are some baseline things that we should consider when it comes to wellness and well-being as you partner with yourself. As a start, you should know your triggers, your limitations, and have an exit strategy.

Know Your Triggers

In her 2021 article "Identifying Your Triggers," Ariadne Platero, LMSW highlights the importance of knowing our triggers to "allow us to anticipate and, eventually, to make decisions that will help to avoid these same pitfalls in the future." She outlines a four-step process that begins with thinking of a situation where you experienced a conversation or disagreement that triggered immediate anger or reactive behavior. Once you identify a scenario, the next step is to break it down into parts. This requires replaying the incident in a way that allows you to chunk it down by the setting, the tones used, the subject, the context, and even the volume of the exchange. You should also think about the circumstances leading up to the incident, such as how you were feeling that day, your state of mind, how much rest you'd had the night before, and the like. All of this will help you contextualize your reaction. After clarifying the what of the situation, you'll need some time to reflect as honestly as possible about the reasons things impacted you and why. The final step is to decide on what you can do with the information. I would add that you consider what is within your control. We can only influence others, but we can choose how we react to them. The bottom line here is that you will be triggered; give yourself the best opportunity to navigate it well by understanding what could pose a challenge to your ability to respond well.

Understand Your Limitations

Even when we have a fair understanding of our triggers, we all have our own internal threshold of what we can handle well. That's why it is incumbent upon us to be honest about what reaching our limits looks and feels like, so we know when to walk away. I recall an incident that took place during a meeting I was co-facilitating where someone took the liberty of being openly disrespectful by yelling at me and my co-facilitator, an incredibly triggering moment that pushed me to the limits of my capacity to engage with the room. I completed the immediate task then left the room to cool off; had I stayed in the room, I might have responded in a way that I would certainly have regretted. Although I didn't address the situation in the moment, I took the evening to reflect on how I wanted to address it and did so the following morning, when cooler heads prevailed.

Have an Exit Strategy

Knowing when to walk away is as important as determining when to partner. Having an exit strategy is not something that tends to be top of mind for many of us, but you'll need to think about when a partnership is too costly to your project, team, and overall well-being.

Part of detaching from a partnership may require identifying another person who may be able to provide the information, insights, or resources you need, and if that's not possible, knowing what you might do without that need being met. Part of your exit strategy might also entail you asking someone else to engage with the person or group you're detaching from. By taking this approach, you are in a good position to both relieve the stress triggered by the interaction and to obtain the desired outcomes or resources.

References

Baertlein, L. (2011) Starbucks: Kraft interfering with grocery transition. Reuters, www.reuters.com/article/idUSTRE7064Y0/ (archived at https://perma.cc/THP3-C463)

Brown, A. and Williams, B. (2019). Team building through social activities: A case study. *Journal of Organizational Psychology*, 24 (3), 112–28.

Brzustewicz, P., Escher, I., Hatami, A., Hermes, J., Keränen, A., and Ulkuniemi, P. (2022). Emergence of social impact in company–NGO relationships in corporate volunteering. *Journal of Business Research*, 140, 62–75.

Burke, W. W. and Noumair, D. A. (2015). *Organization Development: A Process of Learning and Changing*. Pearson Education.

Carasco, M. (2021). Leveraging applied behavioral science in business settings: The field of organization development. *Psi Chi*, 26 (2) the International Honor Society in Psychology.

Carasco, M. and Rothwell, W. J. (2020). *The Essential HR Guide for Small Businesses and Startups: Best Practices, Tools, Examples, and Online Resources*. Society for Human Resource Management

Eskerod, P. and Jepsen, A.L. (2013). *Project Stakeholder Management*. Routledge.

Georgetown (2023) Online certificate in social impact partnerships, https://scs.georgetown.edu/programs/500/certificate-in-social-impact-partnerships/ (archived at https://perma.cc/4VYP-56W5)

Gilbert, J. (2009). The sandwich generation: The emerging role of middle managers in organizational change. Paper presented at PMI® Global Congress 2009—North America, Orlando, FL. Newtown Square, PA: Project Management Institute.

Google (2023) Our values in action, https://about.google/values-in-action/impact-challenge/ (archived at https://perma.cc/FMC3-62T2)

Garcia, R. and Martinez, S. (2020). The impact of social interactions on workplace stress: A longitudinal analysis. *Journal of Occupational Health Psychology*, **35** (2), 87–103.

Healey J. R. and Woodyard, C. (2013). GM, Ford to jointly develop 10-speed transmissions. *USA Today*, www.usatoday.com/story/money/cars/2013/04/15/ford-general-motors-gm-transmissions/2083485/ (archived at https://perma.cc/AR5P-HHEK)

IBM (2023) Impact report, www.ibm.com/ibm/responsibility/downloads/initiatives/COF03011USEN-CorpSvcCorps.PDF (archived at https://perma.cc/SP9E-75QE)

Jaser, Z. (2021). The real value of middle managers. *Harvard Business Review*, https://hbr.org/2021/06/the-real-value-of-middle-managers (archived at https://perma.cc/CF3E-YQ2K)

Jones, M. et al. (2017). Social support and mental health in the workplace: A meta-analysis. *Journal of Applied Psychology*, **42** (4), 465–82.

Lee, J. and Kim, Y. (2019). Social activities and organizational attractiveness: The mediating role of perceived company culture. *Journal of Applied Social Psychology*, **29** (1), 53–68.

Leswing, K. (2020). Apple is breaking a 15-year partnership with Intel on its Macs—here's why. CNBC, www.cnbc.com/2020/11/10/why-apple-is-breaking-a-15-year-partnership-with-intel-on-its-macs-.html (archived at https://perma.cc/G6K3-K5XT)

MasterClass (August 30, 2022). What does a chief of staff do? Job description and duties, www.masterclass.com/articles/what-does-a-chief-of-staff-do (archived at https://perma.cc/9N7M-Y2CS)

Meta (2023). Introducing the new Ray Ban/Meta smart glasses, https://about.fb.com/news/2023/09/new-ray-ban-meta-smart-glasses/ (archived at https://perma.cc/4LXB-WSTB

Panasonic (2023). Panasonic strengthens collaboration with Tesla by $30 million investment, https://news.panasonic.com/global/topics/4421 (archived at https://perma.cc/X4R7-JAMN)

Platero, A. (February 26, 2021). Identifying your triggers. *Psychology Today*, www.psychologytoday.com/us/blog/reflect-and-reset/202102/identifying-your-triggers (archived at https://perma.cc/8JQ4-PZ4H)

Roberts, H. and Anderson, L. (2018). The role of social interactions in shaping organizational culture. *Academy of Management Journal*, **41** (5), 678–94.

Salesforce (2023) Stakeholder Impact Report, https://stakeholderimpactreport.salesforce.com/about-salesforce (archived at https://perma.cc/TPE2-BPZX)

Smith, P. and Johnson, R. (2018). The impact of workplace social activities on job satisfaction. *Journal of Applied Behavioral Science*, **36** (2), 145–62.

Thompson, G. and Davis, C. (2016). Social engagement and employee commitment: A longitudinal study. *Journal of Business and Psychology*, **20** (3), 287–301.

Unilever (2023). www.unilever.com/our-company/our-history-and-archives/2010-2020/ (archived at https://perma.cc/9BVL-WTWV)

Vinturella, J. and Erickson, S. (2013). Determining the amount needed. In *Raising Entrepreneurial Capital (Second Edition)*, www.sciencedirect.com/topics/social-sciences/sales-organization (archived at https://perma.cc/F2VU-TFBM)

8

Elevating the Significance of Employee Resource Groups

According to the Society for Human Resource Management (SHRM):

> Employee resource groups (ERGs), also called affinity groups, are
> employee groups that come together either voluntarily, based on a
> common interest or background, or at the request of a company.
> Examples of common ERGs are those formed around race, ethnicity,
> gender, disability, sexual orientation, parental status, national origin,
> religion or belief, or generation (SHRM, n.d.).

A Brief History of ERGs

In modern society, as citizens become more comfortable in understanding who they are, there may be opportunity to explore an
evolution of the above categories to be even more inclusive:

> The first official ERG (Employee Resource Group) in the United States,
> the Xerox National Black Employees Caucus, was created in 1970
> as a forum for Black employees to advocate for inclusion and change
> within the company. Since that time, ERGs across the United States
> have connected groups of employees who share interests and identities.
> Today, 90 percent of Fortune 500 companies have ERGs (Catalino
> et al., 2022).

According to Welbourne, Rolf, and Schlachter (2015), "In the 1960s, the needs of individuals to be socially connected coincided with the business goals of organizations trying to improve diversity and inclusion within their workforces". Furthermore, "ERGs are sponsored by the organization, but they are staffed by volunteers. Employees who are already working paid jobs take it upon themselves to spend additional unpaid time to help improve the organization by being members of one or more ERGs in their firms". Moreover:

> ERGs provide social and professional support for members (e.g. mentoring programs, visibility with senior leaders), function as a path for advocacy (e.g. help promote learning about their causes and positive change, such as working for equality via LGBT organizations), and provide avenues for information sharing (e.g. programs for black history month, teaching about women leaders, etc.) (p. 5).

I for one am excited at the opportunity to engage with ERG leaders to offer insights that would otherwise not be captured.

Given the more than 50 years since the establishment of the first ERG, there may be a question about their relevance, especially in light of the 2023 United States Supreme Court ruling that makes the consideration of race for college and university admissions problematic. It is believed that this decision will have a ripple effect across the country, and quite frankly it has already started. One example stems from:

> A legal battle between a program that awards grants to female entrepreneurs of color and a conservative nonprofit organization [that raised] broader legal questions on the use of diversity programs in corporate America. The 11th U.S. Circuit Court of Appeals in Atlanta ruled on Saturday to temporarily block the Fearless Fund from running its Strivers Grant Contest, which awards $20,000 grants to small businesses that are led by at least one woman of color and other requirements (Wright, 2023).

Could this be a harbinger of what's to come?

EMPLOYEE RESOURCE GROUPS   141

For the time being, there are still a number of organizations looking to drive impact and shift outcomes in communities that would
benefit from their investment. As of June 2023, in their report on how
they build diversity, equity, and inclusion into their culture, Amazon
highlighted five separate initiatives aimed at supporting underrepresented groups through purposeful investments:

- Amazon Catalytic Capital, a $150 million program to fund
  historically marginalized entrepreneurs.
- The Black Business Accelerator, a $150 million commitment to
  back Black business owners.
- The Impact Accelerator for Women Founders, which provides
  financial backing, networking, and other ongoing support to
  startup founders.
- The AWS Impact Accelerator, a series of programs designed to help
  and support high-potential, pre-seed startups led by underrepresented founders that they have invested $30 million in.
- Amazon's Housing Equity Fund, which provides more than $2 billion
  in below-market loans and grants to preserve and create more than
  20,000 affordable homes for individuals and families earning
  moderate to low incomes in our hometown communities

Through these and other initiatives led by companies with impact
and influence, we might be able to retain and expand these investments rather than move away from them based on fear of loss or a
false narrative that these approaches are no longer needed.

The Obama Effect

When Barack Obama was elected to become the 44th President of
the United States and the first African American person to occupy
that seat, there was a lot of rhetoric around what was believed to
now be a post-racial America. The implications of that ideology
were that racism was a thing of the past; a Black man had been
voted into that office so there was nothing to complain about, no
further work to be done, and certainly no need for affirmative action

initiatives. Optimism was certainly in the air in a way that I had never experienced before. I was traveling during the 2008 election and watched the results from my hotel room in Spain. In the days that followed, I continued my vacation in the region and made my way to Gibraltar and Morocco. I was accompanied by two other women of color who bore witness to and experienced what we could only attribute to the election of Barack Obama. In one incident, we were on a chartered tour bus making our way deeper into Morocco. Several local men who may have been security personnel entered the bus and gave us the most unusual greeting. They bowed their heads and said "Obama." It was strange and exhilarating at the same time. With that single gesture, there was an acknowledgment and awareness that we were Americans and that we were connected to something bigger than us. It was an acknowledgment that something powerful had propagated around the world, and we were respected as a result. I was experiencing what felt like a real sentiment of hope.

Yet in the years after President Obama left office, the United States continued to experience division amongst racial groups. Headlines have been littered with narratives and experiences of racial injustice stemming from police brutality, violence against members of the Asian community during the pandemic, and a litany of other incidents of injustice. On January 6, 2021, a powder keg of anger cloaked in extreme nationalism and frustration galvanized at the United States Capitol in a riot. After the incident, the Federal Bureau of Investigation (FBI) announced a search for participants and shared photos and videos to aid in the search. They stated:

> The FBI is seeking the public's assistance in identifying individuals who made unlawful entry into the U.S. Capitol building and committed various other alleged criminal violations, such as destruction of property, assaulting law enforcement personnel, targeting members of the media for assault, and other unlawful conduct, on January 6, 2021, in Washington, D.C. (FBI, n.d.).

This was serious, and in the years that followed, court hearings were held and many participants received prison sentences for their participation in the riot. The Capitol riots are one of the most glaring examples of the enduring work needed on race relations in the United States.

Deloitte's Radical Decision on ERGs

In 2017, Deloitte took a radical approach to diversity work in their organization when they decided to phase out ERGs and use inclusion councils instead:

> The firm is ending its women's network and other affinity groups and starting to focus on... men. The central idea: It'll offer all managers— including the white guys who still dominate leadership—the skills to become more inclusive, then hold them accountable for building more balanced businesses (Wittenberg-Cox, 2017).

The rationale for this approach was essentially that "these networks divide people up into artificial subgroups (which group does a Black lesbian join?) and isolate them from the networks of power and influence that are such a key part of how leaders identify and promote people" (Wittenberg-Cox, 2017). Instead, the inclusion councils would create a space for all employees to be welcomed. What became of those shifts? And what were the implications for those underrepresented groups?

In the years since their initial announcement to shift the ways of engaging with ERGs, Deloitte may have only rebranded themselves in the areas of diversity and inclusion. According to their 2021 DEI transparency report, their inclusion strategy for meaningful employee experiences is grounded in two main anchors: inclusion councils and what they refer to as business resource groups (BRGs). People from various businesses, roles, identities, and experiences often participate in activities centered around inclusion, development, and community impact through inclusion councils. Events are centered around shared hobbies and interests and can take many different forms, such as mental health awareness, anti-racism reading clubs, brave talks, taking part in local Pride events, and tutoring in schools. Business resource groups (BRGs) comprise formal chapters such as the Asian BRG, the Black Employee Network, Ability First, the Deloitte Parents

Network, the Women's Network (WIN), the International BRG, GLOBE & Allies (LGBTQIA+), the Black Employee Network, the Armed Forces BRG, and several informal chapters. The report also indicated Deloitte's plan to work more closely with BRGs for a better understanding of the experiences of their team members and to increase the connection between BRGs and inclusion councils for empowerment and allyship.

It appears to me that Deloitte rebranded the ERG label, kept the identity-based groups, and added inclusion councils for a broader all-around comprehensive approach to employee experiences. There is something to be said about branding these groups. For example, at GitHub, ERGs are referred to as communities of belonging (CoBs). When compared to the label *employee resource group*, there is a shift in sentiment and understanding of the purpose of the group, albeit with overlap. The Cambridge Online Dictionary defines the word *belong* as "to be in the right place or suitable place, and to feel happy or comfortable in a situation." Contrast that with the word *resource*, which means "something that can be used to help you." I would certainly prefer to feel a sense of belonging instead of anchoring my sentiments in what I can get out of being in a group. But that's me, and a personal preference, and demonstrates just how important labels and marketing are. Don't get me wrong, it shouldn't end there. Having a clear and meaningful purpose is that much more important, and there isn't a one-size-fits-all approach, but what I have observed are some patterns in the ways many companies have engaged with ERGs and the opportunities I see to partner differently. But before we go there, let's unpack some of the reasons why diversity initiatives fail.

Some Reasons Why Diversity Initiatives Fail

In a study conducted by Dobbin and Kalev (2016), they found that many of the challenges with diversity initiatives are that "organizations are trying to reduce bias with the same kinds of programs they've been using since the 1960s. And the usual tools—diversity training, hiring tests, performance ratings, grievance systems—tend to make things worse, not better." What I've noticed is that there is a bit of a copy-paste mindset when it comes to diversity work. Companies peer over the proverbial fence to see what their corporate neighbors are doing and take steps to keep up with the Joneses or the those doing research on the Joneses. We are in the first century of the third millennium—where's the originality? Who's willing to be creative, adaptive, and truly inclusive in developing something transformational? Where is the innovation in diversity, equity, and inclusion? I believe that if we lean into the principles of organization development and tap into the hearts and minds of the people in our organization, innovative ideas will come.

As you might imagine, most organizations aren't taking this approach, and so the list of reasons why diversity initiatives fail keeps growing. But before I add my two cents, I want to highlight the work of Davidson (2011), who outlines nine reasons why diversity approaches are failing:

1 Traditional approaches to managing differences in organizations— Managing Diversity approaches—are less and less effective in our new global marketplace.

2 Having greater diversity in an organization doesn't always translate into superior outcomes.

3 Benefits of diversity are easier to see when looking at team performance, but only for certain kinds of differences. Diversity related to work tasks—diversity of functions, expertise, or tenure— leads to greater team productivity and stronger rapport than does diversity of race, gender, or age.

4 People don't automatically like working together when they feel divided by difference. Introducing some kinds of diversity can diminish commitment and increase turnover.

5 Hiring for diversity is difficult because organizations don't look in the right places, the jobs they are recruiting for aren't always well defined, and even if job responsibilities are clear and the right people are available, biases can prevent managers from hiring them.

6 Retaining people who are different is challenging, because organizational cultures and practices aren't always designed to support them, and because majority employees—white men, in the US-focused studies we surveyed—aren't always comfortable in more diverse settings.

7 Resistance persists, and learning about difference suffers because of it.

8 Managing Diversity approaches haven't succeeded in delivering better outcomes for a number of reasons:

  a. They can limit the very people they are designed to help by spotlighting them and making them the focus of stereotyping and role-slotting.

  b. Fear about fully engaging difference stifles collaboration and keeps people from building effective working relationships.

  c. Managing Diversity activities aren't well suited to effect long-term change, promoting "quick-win" approaches that lead to short-term change without ongoing transformation.

9 Managing Diversity approaches often do not effectively counter resistance. They have lost the attention of both advocates and detractors, discouraging people of difference and making diversity seem less relevant as an organizational issue.

My Two Cents on Why Diversity Initiatives Fail

Some of these challenges highlighted by Davidson are fairly difficult to stomach, especially the notion that *having greater diversity in an organization doesn't always translate into superior outcomes.* Can you imagine making the case for diversity work without anchoring it in better outcomes for the business? If not anchored in that, then in what? And why do this at all? Of course, there are a number of other reasons to engage in diversity initiatives. But what if it was anchored in something as simple as a desire to reflect the world in which we live and work? Very few employees and leaders would be motivated by that. Two reasons I've found that these initiatives go nowhere are *lack of connection to business strategy* and *zero accountability (rewards or punitive measures)* for moving it forward. This is business 101, management by objectives, so why don't we hold people accountable for real? I think it's because we don't want to make them uncomfortable. Now this is going to ruffle more than a few feathers, but the work of Tema Okun (which is often misused) on the ways White supremacy culture can appear in organizations highlights *the right to comfort* as one of those ways. It is in fact "the belief that those with power have a right to emotional and psychological comfort" (2001, p. 7). With this understanding we can surmise at least onto institutionalized ideologies that can get in the way of real progress.

Another reason that I believe diversity initiatives fail is *diversity leader exclusion* and *burnout*. You read that right: leaders trying to move inclusion initiatives get excluded, sometimes overtly, when those in positions of power or influence downplay the reality of the employee experiences or the climate in the company, or in more subtle ways like shortening their time on a meeting call or delaying and rescheduling meetings that were needed to move initiatives further along.

These and similar actions harken to other elements of the right to comfort mentioned earlier but, in this case, it involves "scapegoating those who cause discomfort, equating individual acts of unfairness against white people with systemic racism which daily targets people of color" (Okun, 2001). There is something here about preserving power through punitive measures. Moreover, these actions also represent what Okun refers to as *power hoarding*, where there is little to no value placed on sharing power, and it is believed that there is only so much of it to go around. Those in positions of authority also perceive themselves as being in charge and feel threatened when others suggest making changes to the way things are done in the company. They also believe that those in positions of power are acting in the organization's best interests and believe that those who are calling for change are inexperienced, emotional, and ill-informed. The result of power hoarding is exclusion, and the impact of power hoarding is exhaustion ultimately leading to the creation of a figurehead or *constructive dismissal*, a term used more frequently outside of the United States, meaning being forced to leave a position due to the employer's actions. In the United States, the more common term is *constructive discharge*, which "occurs when working conditions are made so unbearable or abusive that a reasonable person believes that resignation is the only appropriate action for them to take" (SHRM, n.d.).

At the end of the day, you are forced out. Forced to abandon your vision for the organization and into subjection to the status quo or forced leave. Without addressing the root issues, the alternative is to be like Sisyphus, who, in Greek mythology, "is punished in the underworld by the god Zeus, who forces him to roll a boulder up a hill for eternity. Every time he nears the top of the hill, the boulder rolls back down" (Britannica, 2023). This is an endless loop of fruitless action and a prerequisite to burnout. The work required in this space is emotionally taxing, especially when led by people of color, but add to it hamster wheel experiences and you then have a recipe to disrupt wellness and any possibility of progress.

Activity-based Diversity Initiatives

When I first joined the corporate world, one of the things that I thought was very interesting was seeing groups within an organization that were created to be spaces for various minority groups to connect. The value of that space may be different from one person to another, but I could say, for myself, having worked in predominantly White institutions, and also having attended predominantly White colleges and universities, a space where I could engage with people that at least shared one demographic was not only needed but, at the time, healing. Now, this is by no means the same thing, but I want to mention that when I attended AfroTech, the largest Black technology conference in the world, it was one of those moments where I felt the most comfortable in a professional conference setting. It's strange to say this now, because I feel like I am someone who is myself in every setting, but I had no thought about filtering aspects of myself in that setting, barring the usual stranger danger. There was a collective sigh of relief and appreciation for the value that we all brought into that space. It could've been the fact in the two years post-Covid, coming out of isolation and quarantine, there was a great need to connect with others who were like us and had experienced similar challenges but were equally eager to celebrate the fact that we were here, alive and thriving in tech, and able to connect in ways that we had not done in the years prior. ERGs can serve a very similar purpose as relates to a space of belonging for marginalized communities to feel seen and safe. But at the end of the day, they are housed in corporations within broader organization systems that come with their own political strife and power plays.

That aside, what I found to be consistent in terms of the kinds of programs that are offered through ERGs in organizations is those that tend to be connection-based, career-based, activity-based, and celebration-based. There are moments of learning. There are also moments of appreciation and celebration of culture; however, I have yet to see anything connected to the business strategy in an ERG. I believe that the greater opportunity is to leverage the differences in these communities to be more deliberately connected to moving forward the strategic initiatives of the organization, and that requires the business actually taking the time to see the value that each community brings, and the differences in the perspectives that can help the organization be better or different than it currently is. If this approach is embraced, it can provide the level of gravitas needed by ERGs to extend their impact beyond activity-based initiatives to be respected as strategic partners by business leaders and fellow employees.

ERGs as Strategic Partners

According to Rodriguez (2021), "ERGs are quite prevalent in organizations, with approximately 90 percent of the Fortune 500 companies having employee resource groups. Organizations usually have between six to eight employee resource groups with the occasional company having a dozen or more separate ERGs globally." If the system permits, or you're inclined to apply some pressure to make it happen, you can leverage ERGs differently.

At first, the ERG usually concentrates on the social side of the group, aiming to foster a sense of community through networking events and forming relationships with individuals who share similar interests or backgrounds. ERGs gradually broaden their scope to incorporate member career development programs and a greater emphasis on outreach to the outside community. Eventually, they start putting initiatives into action with the intention of better aligning with corporate objectives and business priorities (Rodriguez, 2021). So, what does it take to cultivate ERGs that offer a substantive and enduring impact that extends beyond receiving financial support for events? It starts with who occupies the leadership positions in those groups and prioritizing their development in these roles, along with ERG alignment to the overall business interests in the areas of diversity, equity, and inclusion that have measures of accountability. This will encourage a deeper understanding of their relevance. In other words:

> Alignment with talent management initiatives often involves ensuring that strong performers are in the leadership roles of the ERGs. If the employee resource group does not have a strong leader, companies are now starting to appoint someone to the role of ERG leader who is more capable. The person appointed is increasingly someone who is already deemed a high performer or someone with tremendous potential (Rodriguez, 2021).

Furthermore, your organization will need to also embrace the notion of ERG leaders taking on some governance roles to help shape the success of D&I efforts.

To Pay or Not to Pay, That Is the Question

Now I would be remiss not to mention the issue of paying ERG leaders, which has been a bit of a hot topic in the diversity space for a while. Let's be clear: leading an employee resource group can be very taxing and incredibly time-consuming. Most of the people in these roles are volunteers with a passion to engage in the space and are managing a full-time role at the same time. Not all organizations give

ERGs or ERG leaders the same level of respect, but some have gone so far as to compensate their ERG leaders in recognition of their time and energy, and the strategic roles they play in supporting diversity, equity, and inclusion initiatives.

TWITTER

In October 2020, years before Elon Musk bought the social media platform, Twitter made the decision to compensate the leaders of their business resource groups (BRGs), highlighting:

> Our Business Resource Groups (BRGs) are the lifeblood of inclusion efforts at Twitter… and all our BRG chairs around the world— empower our next generation of leaders, foster a culture of inclusivity and belonging, and give back to the greater community. In addition to performing their core job function, they navigate the complexities, nuances, and emotional labor of sometimes being **the only** person who looks, loves, worships, or has lived like them (Twitter, 2020).

This acknowledgment from Dalana Brand, Vice President of People Experience and Head of Inclusion and Diversity at Twitter at the time, is huge! This work often comes with a heavy burden and significant emotional tax and tends to be without empathy. Brand went on to say that "this work is essential to Twitter's success—it is not a 'side hustle' or 'volunteer activity.' That's why we recently introduced a new compensation program to formally recognize the global leadership team of all of our BRGs" (Twitter, 2020)

LINKEDIN

In 2021, Teuila Hanson, Chief People Officer at LinkedIn, acknowledged this when the company established a compensation model for the leaders of their ERGs that would pay $10,000 annually for two-year terms. Hanson said, "Historically, these employees take on leadership roles and the associated work in addition to their day jobs, putting in extra time, energy, and insight. And despite the tremendous value, visibility, and impact to the organization, this work is rarely rewarded financially" (Kramer, 2021). This audacious move on Hanson's part I believe should be applied to all ERGs in all organizations. Even if the business allocates a small stipend, it sends the right message regarding the level of seriousness and value ERGs have as partners in supporting the business.

AUTODESK

Also in 2021, AutoDesk recognized the impact and contributions of their ERG leaders during 2020, a year of global intensity on issues of race-based violence. Rita Giacalone, former VP, Culture, Diversity and Talent Development at AutoDesk, highlighted that "2021 represents an inflection point at Autodesk as a company, for leadership and for employees. The issue of racial justice in America was brought to the forefront in 2020 with the deaths of George Floyd, Breonna Taylor, Ahmaud Arbery, and others." This acknowledgment led to the decision for the company to compensate their ERG leaders through "an appreciation bonus of $10,000, or the local currency equivalent. The bonus will be given annually in April, upon completion of each year of full service as an ERG lead" (AutoDesk, 2021).

DOORDASH

In 2022, DoorDash, one of the most popular food delivery companies, also made the decision to compensate the leaders of their eight official ERGs, "because of their significance in shaping what life at DoorDash is like [and] for their time and invaluable contributions" (DoorDash, 2022). Vanessa Chui, Manager of Employee Connections at DoorDash, highlights that

> Employee Resource Groups are deeply important to the foundation of our culture. This work takes thought, effort, and dedication as our leaders tackle business problems and help their communities thrive. Investing in underrepresented talent is critical to us serving our employees and customers better and creating a truly equitable workplace (DoorDash, 2022).

To engage ERG leaders as strategic partners, companies will need to shift their mindset about these groups and engage them as serious connectors and enablers across the business. After that, they will need to establish some rigor around who gets to lead an ERG, invest in their development specifically as leaders of ERGs, and compensate them for the work they will do in this space.

Other Practical Matters in Elevating the ERG Leaders to Strategic DEI Partners

If your organization has created a process to select an ERG leader, and by proxy executive sponsors for each group, prioritized leadership training specific to the needs of these groups, and budgeted to compensate ERG leaders for their work, you're in great shape. But all of this must be anchored in a clearly defined DEI strategy tightly coupled with the business vision and direction in a given year *with* metrics and measures of accountability. Again, manage by objectives. Taking these steps is critical and foundational, and in my view by no means optional. These steps also send a very strong message to everyone in the organization that diversity, equity, inclusion, and belonging are serious organization priorities. Your organization is then well positioned to garner the support of ERGs as strategic partners.

Other Important Actions to Build Partnership

I can't overestimate the power of inclusion when we talk about strengthening partnerships. From my experience in some organizations, senior leaders and members of the human resources team are viewed as talking heads, frequently sticking to the robotic script of business speak and a multitude of vagaries. This leads to a lack of trust. To fix this, your company needs to leverage as many opportunities as possible to be forthcoming and transparent, especially with the leaders of your ERGs. You can do this by providing previews and or opportunities to weigh in on future changes. One example of when an opportunity to weigh in was helpful came from a neuro-based ERG that had previously expressed frustration with the complexity in the wording of HR announcements. To mitigate this, leaders in this neuro-based ERG were invited to review and edit the language in an upcoming communication, which was valuable to both the members of that neurodivergent community and the organization at large. I have also witnessed firsthand just how important and impactful a preview can be when a company chose not to provide a preview of a health benefit change to members of the trans community, particularly those who were using the old benefit. The fallout was ugly, and those impacted expressed frustration with not being consulted, especially those who accounted for specific care (such as scheduled surgeries with clarity on the financial responsibility). The new benefit would place them in a position of uncertainty with timing of surgery and new costs. Though a small population in the organization, the trans community deserved to have more time for this benefit change. Let me say that not all leaders are going to agree with me on this, in fact many do not. I'm not saying to give previews or provide weigh-ins on everything; what I am proposing are more deliberate and thoughtful considerations around the impact of what might seem like minor business decisions. Changing trans healthcare benefits? Consider talking with members of the LGBTQIA+ community in a focus group. If this step had been taken in the aforementioned company, the concerns that erupted after the benefits change could have been mitigated, and the actual value of the old benefit would have been realized.

Another way your organization can cultivate better strategic partnerships with ERG leaders is to leverage them in cascading messages on change initiatives deeper in the organization. Let me be clear: you shouldn't expect these leaders to do so just because they are ERG leaders—that would be an unethical quid pro quo. However, if you've garnered the respect and trust of the ERG leaders in your organization and provided opportunities for their voices to not only be heard, but leveraged, you are more likely to have partners willing to support change management. One of the ways they might do so is by sharing content within their respective ERGs before the broader company.

ERG Summits

One of my favorite ways of deepening that strategic partnership is to host an ERG Summit. "Since about 2015, there has been a significant increase in the number of companies that now hold an annual leadership summit for their ERG leaders. These summits run anywhere from four hours to four days" Rodriguez (2021). More than just an opportunity to gather, ERG leadership summits are a powerful catalyst to connect ERG leaders to strategic collaborative opportunities across ERGs and the broader organization. How does it work? Well, typically, these summits bring together ERG leaders to hear from business executives, discover goals related to diversity and inclusion, network with other ERG leaders, participate in panels with ERG leaders from other businesses, and so on, and require significant investment by the organization. The companies that do not hold their own ERG summits send their ERG leaders to external organizations' events as a professional development benefit. An ERG summit can bring all of the aforementioned pieces together annually to anchor the direction of the planning and partnership over the course of the year.

Leader Commitment, Buy-in, and Accountability

Leader Commitment

None of this matters without leader commitment, buy-in, and accountability. Therefore, it is the responsibility of company executives to ensure that ERGs are in line with both the business's DEI priorities and employee expectations. Experience indicates that this task can be completed by focusing on a number of elements, including making sure that the objectives and goals of each ERG are well communicated, coordinating each ERG's activities with the corporate DEI plan, and providing enough organizational support for the ERG leaders. (Catalino et al., 2022): "Amazing ideas alone do not convert into transformation, member pleasure, or great experiences, as with every group or new endeavor." Several recurrent success criteria have been identified through research on ERGs and member surveys. The five ERG factors identified by McKinsey & Company that correlate to employees' sense of inclusion and belonging are one noteworthy discovery. These aspects include community development among employees, allyship, leadership connections, external participation, and career advancement (Reshwan, 2023). I'd like to spend some time on the leadership connections aspect.

People in positions of power aren't very keen on giving it up, irrespective of how noble the cause is. Partnerships will require time and resources. You'll need to give those with positional power a reason to engage. The proverbial "what's in it for me?" question must be answered on their end. It's not something that tends to be said out loud, but just know that people aren't going to risk their positional power, control of narratives, or social equity to help you. That's the reality: they need to be incentivized. "A number of companies have gotten consistently positive results with tactics that don't focus on control. They apply three basic principles: engage managers in solving the problem, expose them to people from different groups, and encourage social accountability for change" (Dobbin and Kalev, 2016).

Leader Accountability

Tema Okun's work on White supremacist culture highlights another concept that I believe can be applied to our understanding of what can get in the way of progress in partnering with ERGS: power hoarding. When in action there is a sentiment of

> little, if any, value around sharing power; power seen as limited, only so much to go around; those with power feel threatened when anyone suggests changes in how things should be done in the organization, feel suggestions for change are a reflection on their leadership; those with power don't see themselves as hoarding power or as feeling threatened; those with power assume they have the best interests of the organization at heart and assume those wanting change are ill-informed (stupid), emotional, inexperienced (Okun, 2001).

As difficult as that was to read myself, I can attest to Okun's description in my own lived experience doing both organization development and diversity work in a number of organizations that left me feeling like I was not only spinning my wheels but wasting my time—part of the emotional tax that professionals in this line of business can attest to.

Okun gives us a few antidotes to consider:

include power sharing in your organization's values statement; discuss what good leadership looks like and make sure people understand that a good leader develops the power and skills of others; understand that change is inevitable and challenges to your leadership can be healthy and productive; make sure the organization is focused on the mission (Okun, 2001).

Furthermore, some antidotes to the right to comfort which can show us as scapegoating those who cause discomfort are:

understand that discomfort is at the root of all growth and learning; welcome it as much as you can; deepen your political analysis of racism and oppression so you have a strong understanding of how your personal experience and feelings fit into a larger picture; don't take everything personally (Okun, 2001).

Easier said than done, right? But I sometimes wonder if the issues that diversity, equity, and inclusion professionals are trying to tackle within an organization are much deeper issues that can't be addressed through the tools we provide or the interventions we attempt to introduce. Our approaches simply are not sufficient because of the deeper work needed to resolve the root causes of these dysfunctional behaviors in people and systems in organizations. What am I saying? There is a deeper work required by every individual in an organization to become functional empathetic human beings able to both manage themselves and respect the value and presence of others—an idea which actually sparks what could be quite the pivot for me in terms of my engagement with organizations.

But until such time, as we have mental health professionals supporting the actual development and healing work, needed not only by leaders but by individual contributors and organizations, what can we do? I mentioned this earlier, but the concept of managing by objectives is incredibly important, especially in corporate environments where individuals may be driven by goals or rewards. Therefore, having measures of accountability connected to any strategic business initiative, including leader commitments to supporting equity work within an organization, is paramount. I am of the opinion that accountability measures should not only be individually driven meanings specific to a given leader, but also socially shared. Dobbin and Kalev (2016) tell us that "encouraging social accountability plays on our need to look good in the eyes of those around us." In my view, this is the sort of public shaming that can drive individuals to make change. But let's look at the opposite first. During the autumn season, many organizations tend to have commitments to philanthropy, and encourage their employees to donate to any number of charities, with the organization adding or matching their contributions. A number of groups in the organization may compete with one another to see which group can raise the most money. This kind of public goal setting in this area creates a specific kind of camaraderie and desire to drive goodness forward. In like manner, if certain goals were made public, some organizations, and even groups within organizations, would be more willing and committed to driving change within their business unit or team because of the potential for being shamed publicly for not making commitments or progress in a given area. This is why these goals, and progress toward them, should be made public.

The opportunity to shift the ways your organization connects with and leverages ERGs is a great one. When anchored in strategic initiatives, ERG communities have the opportunity to not only thrive in spaces where they can feel safe and seen, but also to experience a sense of value and contributing to the broader organizational direction. Some shifts are required, including selecting the appropriate individuals to lead an ERG, investing in their leadership development and business acumen, providing compensation for the time spent performing the work, as well as creating specific spaces for senior leaders to thoughtfully engage with ERGs.

References

Amazon (June 5, 2023). In this together: How Amazon builds diversity, equity, and inclusion into its culture, www.aboutamazon.com/news/workplace/inside-amazons-culture-of-inclusion-for-employees-customers-and-communities (archived at https://perma.cc/5AU3-THTK)

AutoDesk (2021). Autodesk announces annual appreciation bonus for Employee Resource Group leads, https://novedge.com/blogs/design-news/autodesk-announces-annual-appreciation-bonus-for-employee-resource-group-leads (archived at https://perma.cc/3EHX-XG4N)

Britannica (2023). Sisyphus, www.britannica.com/topic/Sisyphus (archived at https://perma.cc/M4MZ-HYMW)

Cambridge Dictionary (2023). Belong, https://dictionary.cambridge.org/dictionary/english/belong (archived at https://perma.cc/FUB2-4DWM)

Catalino, N., Gardner, N., Goldstein, D. and Wong, J. (2022) Effective employee resource groups are key to inclusion at work. Here's how to get them right. McKinsey & Company, www.mckinsey.com/capabilities/people-and-organizational-performance/our-insights/effective-employee-resource-groups-are-key-to-inclusion-at-work-heres-how-to-get-them-right (archived at https://perma.cc/453U-BSMY)

Davidson, M. N. (2011) *The End of Diversity As We Know It : Why Diversity Efforts Fail and How Leveraging Difference Can Succeed*. Berrett-Koehler.

Deloitte (2021) 2021 Transparency Report, www2.deloitte.com/content/dam/Deloitte/us/Documents/about-deloitte/dei-transparency-report.pdf (archived at https://perma.cc/42FC-YMRZ)

Dobbin, F. and Kalev, A. (July–August 2016). Why diversity programs fail and what works better. *Harvard Business Review Magazine.*

DoorDash (2022). About Doordash, https://about.doordash.com/en-us/news/doordash-employee-resource-groups-paid-leaders-compensation (archived at https://perma.cc/LZH5-D4MV)

FBI (n.d.) U.S. Capitol Violence, www.fbi.gov/wanted/capitol-violence (archived at https://perma.cc/CUP6-J9TA)

Kramer, A. (2021). LinkedIn will pay $10,000 to its ERG leaders. Protocol, www.protocol.com/bulletins/linkedin-will-pay-10-000-to-erg-leaders (archived at https://perma.cc/R5EZ-73KL)

Okun, T. (2001). *White Supremacy Culture*. DRworks.

Reshwan, R. (June 5, 2023) What Are Employee Resource Groups? US News, https://money.usnews.com/careers/company-culture/articles/what-are-employee-resource-groups (archived at https://perma.cc/78R8-Z5QB)

Rodriguez, R. (2021). *Employee Resource Group Excellence: Grow High Performing ERGs to Enhance Diversity, Equality, Belonging, and Business Impact*. John Wiley & Sons.

SHRM (n.d.) HR Glossary, www.shrm.org/topics-tools/tools/hr-glossary (archived at https://perma.cc/M4WM-PCHE)

Twitter (2020) Inclusion & Diversity Report September 2020: #BlackLivesMatter, https://blog.twitter.com/en_us/topics/company/2020/inclusion-and-diversity-report-blacklivesmatter-september-2020 (archived at https://perma.cc/F5D3-UHSF)

Welbourne, T. M., Rolf, S., and Schlachter, S. (2015). Employee resource groups: An introduction, review and research agenda, Center for Effective Organizations, https://ceo.usc.edu/wp-content/uploads/2015/05/2015-13-G15-13-660-ERG_Introduction_Review_Research.pdf (archived at https://perma.cc/24GN-ZF5C)

Wittenberg-Cox, A. (2017). Deloitte's radical attempt to reframe diversity. *Harvard Business Review*, https://hbr.org/2017/08/deloittes-radical-attempt-to-reframe-diversity (archived at https://perma.cc/ZX93-C3FX)

Wright, K. (2023). A federal appeals court blocks a grant program for Black female entrepreneurs. NPR, www.npr.org/2023/10/03/1203221945/affirmative-action-black-female-entrepreneurs (archived at https://perma.cc/C83T-X7QJ)

9

Bringing It All Together

An In-Depth Case Study on Organization Culture Transformation at Fitbit (Now Part of Google)

An Interview Between Marie Carasco and Jaison Williams

Marie

Jaison

This chapter is the culmination of the book and presents a fabulous case study of Fitbit's culture transformation, specifically the most pertinent elements, steps, and mindsets needed to guide you from start to finish in the shortest, most realistic timeframe. At the end of the chapter, I offer some insight into Google's acquisition of Fitbit as a strategic move into the wearable technology industry.

The following is a transcribed interview between the author, Marie Carasco, and Jaison Williams, who at the time of writing is the SVP, Talent Management, Capabilities and Culture at Expedia Group. Before Expedia, he was the VP of Talent Management and Inclusion for Fitbit (now part of Google) and has held global positions with Alight Solutions (formerly Aon Hewitt), GlaxoSmithKline, Pfizer,

American Express, Cendant, and Accenture. He has expertise in inclusion and diversity, learning and leadership development, talent and performance management, and engagement.

Jaison Williams ignites passion and purpose in organizations by designing human-centered approaches that improve how employees experience the workplace—whether in physical or virtual environments. He combines business savvy with a strong execution orientation in a way that boosts employee engagement and performance. His people and organization strategies are both practical and innovative, garnering him accolades as someone who "unlocks" potential and enables companies to reach new levels. Jaison is a frequent speaker, panelist, and session facilitator on the topics of talent and performance management, employee engagement, and inclusion and diversity. He is also a highly sought-after career mentor and coach to mid- and senior-level professionals.

In addition to his executive career, Jaison serves as President of the Board of Directors for the Bloomsburg University (PA) Alumni Association and is a board member of the Stevenson Foundation (IL) and the Evanston (IL) Alumni Chapter of Kappa Alpha Psi Fraternity, Inc. He also mentors students from underrepresented groups at Evanston (IL) High School. Jaison lives with his wife and youngest son in the suburbs of Chicago.

Marie: So our conversation today, Jaison, I'm super excited to have with you as one of the chapters in this book—the final chapter where things are coming together, discussing what I hope would be a holistic framework for transforming organizational culture. I'm delighted to have an opportunity to learn from your experiences at Fitbit, and the transformation work that you were able to achieve. So I first wanted to start by asking about what your role was at Fitbit and how you became involved in culture transformation work, and what was the impetus for the work that you were involved with?

Jaison: Yes, so my role at Fitbit, I was the Vice President of Talent Management, Learning, DEI—I think we just called it talent and diversity to make it short. Those were probably, I guess, the primary things—talent, learning, DEI—so that was my official title. And my role in culture was... Actually, I'd say from the beginning, that was the hook that got me in is that there was this successful... You can call Fitbit a startup, they were probably around 10 years old or so when I started working with them. And they had done everything that you'd want, right? They created an industry, you have two entrepreneurs who now had a publicly traded company that was known worldwide. But there were aspects of the organization that had not been invested in. And frankly may or may not have been in the tool house of the leaders and some of the people that they had hired previously.

So culture was really my remit, and to tell you how early on I knew this, when I interviewed with the CEO James, I said, "James, what's the one thing that you need me to deliver for you in year one?" And he said, "Performance management." Performance management is the foundation in many ways of how cultures operate, right? It reinforces behaviors, the ones we like, and it hopefully shuns the ones that we don't feel are appropriate. It creates a rhythm in the organization around how conversations happen, how feedback happens, so that's one of those things. While there was a company, while there was a culture, there were some foundational elements that were still needed to help the culture really reach its potential.

Marie: Quite interesting. So when you began to understand the needs specific to the culture shift, what were some of the things that you noticed initially as you began to do your diagnostic work around this shift?

Jaison: I would ask myself, how did a company become this globally well known, right? So as an example, I put together the first diversity strategy. There were thoughts, there was even, kind of, I'll call it two ERGs. Really employees were doing diversity; leadership was not doing diversity. It was really one broad group—and then there was a Pride ERG. Even though there was no diversity leader, they would just go petition to get funds to do stuff. So it was very much employee led, but there was not a strategy that went from recruitment, through to learning, through to succession, what have you, so things like that were missing.

They didn't have one performance management practice; there were some groups that had performance management from other companies. So if someone joined from Amazon, and they came in and they said, "Oh, there's no performance management here. Well, I'm just going to do what I did at Amazon." Right? All the way down to groups where people told me, "Hey, my manager just says, 'Hey, here's what your pay increase is. Here's what your RSUs are.'" They didn't have any conversation, they would just get a salary increase with nothing. So there were many things that were blatantly visible—the company didn't have any values, right? And so I didn't have to go necessarily looking to go, "What's missing?" It was in many ways easily observable.

We have a company that in many ways was born of the internet boom, if you can call it that. We didn't have online learning. It was easy to spot some of the things that were missing; we really weren't doing anything in terms of engagement survey. I think when I got there, maybe they had actually just finished… I started in January, and I think in October, November before I joined, they had just completed their first engagement survey.

But there was just a lot of opportunity around because I could see the things that were missing and I understood how if all of those things were addressed or brought to life, it would help with the culture.

Marie: So how did you decide where to start?

Jaison: A little bit through getting my hand smacked, and a little bit through actually listening. The first place I had support and sponsorship for was performance management, so that really became the first place of focus for me. I got my hand slapped when I said, "Well, we need values." And then they said, "Well, why do we need values? We created an industry that didn't exist. We sold a number of devices. We're improving the lives of hundreds of millions of people. And we did that all without having words on the wall that tell us who we are." How do you challenge that? Right?

"Okay, well I'm not going to focus over there." So performance management was the first place I started. And at the same time, I'd probably say it was 75, 80 percent effort was around getting a performance management model framework that the senior leadership was supportive of. And the other part of my time was actually spent trying to figure out, where do we go? What do we do with diversity and inclusion? Which we actually later changed to I and D because the employees felt, "Jaison, in order to attract and retain diverse talent, we first have to have an inclusive culture. So why are we leading with the word diversity as opposed to leading with the word inclusion?" Those were the first two areas of focus for me.

Marie: So I love what you brought up just now, this sort of employee influence shift in the naming. In the sense of this sort of bottom-up swell of impact and insights to inform change. Perhaps I'll have some more questions about employees a little bit later on. But as you began to get clear on your initial areas to focus on and started making some shifts even in the naming convention, what were the key, I would say, frameworks that you leveraged to begin to inform how you would do the work, if you had any? Or was there a different process that you had to help you navigate the various pieces of the transformation process?

Jaison: I'd say for performance management, I definitely looked at what was happening externally. Well, A, you needed to know, and B, what was happening externally had to be in consideration for what was presented to what I'll tell you was called the design council. And at the advice of my chief people officer, I got three members of the executive team who were supportive of things around leadership, culture, et cetera, to be the key stakeholder group that I would present to to say, "Hey, this is the recommendation for ratings, this is the recommendation for potential, this is the..." Right? To get their alignment. And one of the things I quickly realized from looking externally and doing an internal assessment was the external market at this time was oversaturated with companies dropping performance ratings altogether, right? So that was the dominant narrative in 2018, particularly the first half of 2018.

And what I understood from the leaders of the company, from my assessment, was that we didn't have any foundation to go to no ratings. If you have some groups with ratings, some groups with no ratings and others engineering, doing mathematical equations—this person is a 4.1923, right? How do you go from a culture of inconsistency to one of really complete vagueness?

How do you do that without ratings? So it was informed externally, but also driven by me understanding what the needs of the organization were, and really having the voice and input of members of the executive team in order to do that. On the opposite side for inclusion and diversity, that was... And let me pause and just go back. When I was interviewing, the question I asked James of, "What's the one thing you want me to deliver?" (James was the CEO), and James said, "Performance management." So I knew I already had organizational support for that. And I knew that there would be some leadership buy-in to that. With diversity, it was all employee led, so I actually had to start with the employees. I couldn't start with the leadership because that's not where the engagement was, that was not where the energy was. All of that was with a group—gosh, I wish I could remember their name. It'll come to me at some point.

I had to start with the employee group, and basically it was a diversity steering committee of employees. Which kind of was, it wasn't really an ERG, it was more of a steering committee, but there had been a Pride ERG. But very early on in my tenure, the two people who led that left the organization. So for a while there was no Pride ERG, it was really me and the employee steering committee. And really our efforts were really grassroots, really grassroots. How do we create a calendar where we can focus on different diversity events? What's the right word? I can't think of the right... I'm just going to say "causes" because I can't think of the word.

What causes were already of importance for that group of employees? So things like 50/50 Day, that was one of the first things that we focused on. Which is a day focused on how do we get women to parity with men? In terms of pay and everything. This was actually a global 50/50 Day that was one of the first events that we jointly organized, and they had an executive sponsor, and me as the head of DEI. So we focused on just getting some more rhythm around recognition of different months for different groups, et cetera. And at the end of my first year, I actually decided to have a diversity summit. And the diversity summit was me, all the members of... I think I may open it up to say, any employee who's got a passion or is interested that wants to help steer our diversity strategy was invited. I had an external facilitator come in, and I think we did a day and a half or two days to guide us through the process using a lot of design thinking. And that was where the first diversity strategy was birthed.

So from the ground up, not from the bottom up versus the top down. And that's also going back to the earlier story, towards the end of that session, that's when one of the team members said, "Jaison, all the things we've talked about suggest we need an inclusive culture. But we keep talking about diversity and inclusion. So we want to have more diversity in the organization, but if we don't have an inclusive culture, how's that going to happen?" And that was also the impetus. So not only did they have significant input into the strategy, they also reframed how we talked about it as an organization. So those were really the two key focus areas to start shifting the culture, which is that we want to have an inclusive culture, but we want to have one that is high performing as well. So those were the initial steps to start.

The title of the presentation was "Designing a Culture and Engagement Evolution." But when you actually get into the slides, the very second one says, how did Fitbit reboot its culture? These are some of the steps that we took effectively to reboot Fitbit's culture, starting with performance management, then moving into inclusion and diversity. And really driving things around learning and engagement and really how to have a strong focus on employee engagement. Also, this is the time of significant battles for talent in the tech space, particularly for San Francisco–headquartered companies. So yeah, it just started kind of evolving to, "Okay, we've started to make some traction in performance. We're starting to make some traction in inclusion and diversity, let's not rest on our laurels. What are other things that we're hearing?" And again, I mentioned earlier that right before I started, we'd had the first engagement survey.

So by the time I was getting close to a year in the company, I think by that point I had redone the engagement strategy, had run a pulse survey. So we had some more data to help us determine what else to go after. And that's things like focus on learning and making certain every employee had access to learning, and we could start to activate that element of culture. Putting more emphasis for engagement to work, everybody plays a role. And so there was a very deliberate emphasis on what's the role of the manager? What's the role of their team in order to help make progress there? I talk about things in sandwich analogies, I always talk about a change sandwich. To make things successful, if you're making a sandwich, you are not going to have a great sandwich if you just have the top slice of bread, right?

Equally, you're not going to have a great sandwich if you just have the bottom slice of bread, right? But if you've got something in the middle that everyone is working towards and there's efforts coming from the top down, and there's efforts coming from the bottom up, you create ultimately a great sandwich. Because the meat is what you are working towards together.

And that's effectively how a lot of the culture shift and transformation at Fitbit happened. It was a combination of top and bottom meeting together around something in the middle that was valued and there was support for.

Marie: I'm picking up some fundamental pieces for people to pay attention to that there was executive clarity on specific things that were desired outcomes, right? From the very top, as you outlined. And also executive support with the sponsors that connected, but also bottom up, as you described, the lower level of the sandwich. With the employee input, with the steering committee. And also data-driven, leveraging the content from the engagement survey to inform next areas to focus on. And so when you have this really great clarity around the work, it's super helpful. How did you all go from the working groups, the distilling of an output to a socialization across the company for folks to now be able to start to think about this day to day?

Jaison: Almost nothing was done without employee involvement in some way, performance management. We, myself and others, did take it around the company and share it with employees. There were probably small focus groups where we walked them through the things. And that's where I got the direct feedback, "Jaison, why are we going to ratings when everybody else is getting rid of ratings?" And I had to be able to articulate the why behind that. Why are we going to five ratings? Why are we doing this? Because we actually designed it so everyone knew. There was nothing that was not known either by a manager or by an employee—we basically shared with them the exact same information. But everything that we did was informed by some level of leadership, not always the executive, right? And some degree of employee input.

So as I talked about with performance management, I had the design council. The design council was the head of international, the head of the B2B business and the head of design. That was the design council for performance management. At some point, one of the IT leaders, knowing that we wanted to do online learning, said, "Look, we've got our relationship with Workday, we're going in to renegotiate. I think I can get you the LMS module for Workday for free." Right? So we're like, "Okay." So you start getting these advocates who would go, "I believe in what needs to be done." And they would invest some type of capital in it. Matter of fact, that same person, that IT leader who helped us get Workday

Learning also paid for 50 percent of our LinkedIn Learning licenses. So that was his contribution because he was a supporter.

And diversity I had found haphazardly when walking through San Francisco one day. I had found Dev Color, which is a group of Black software engineers. Now, at that time, and I didn't mention this in my intro because it didn't last an extremely long time, but I also led recruiting for pretty much my first year at Fitbit as well. And so I found out about Dev Color, started talking to them, and I was like, "We need to activate this, right? We're saying we want a more diverse workforce, our recruiters..."

But we eventually talked and I felt like there's a relationship here. I went back to one of our engineering leaders and I said, "Look, I really think this is an investment we should make, and I've got the money to cover it in my budget, but I think it would speak volumes if you did."

He said, "Not only will I sponsor it, pay the cost,—Jaison, if we go a year and we get zero hires, I don't care because I don't think that's a failure because we've got to cultivate a relationship, right? Because it's very easy to pay money and rate an organization for their talent."

So while maybe not ideal that there were engineering values and there are company values, because that leader said, "Well, I can't wait for the company to create values. We need some now, they'll help us in recruitment, they'll help us in other things." I was able then to piggyback, gain their advocacy. Because they wanted company values too and were able to get to them. So it's literally been a top down, bottom up. It's never been just kind of one group or one segment of the company, because as part of just even the engineering values, they had individual contributors, right? It couldn't just work for leadership. They had to have a broad representation of the engineering organization to gain agreement on it. So by default, we always had individual contributors, middle managers, senior leaders involved.

Marie: So much collaboration and buy-in from the leadership and sort of putting the money where their mouth is, right? To be deliberate and thoughtful in supporting where the business needed to go. And I love this notion of putting the investment in knowing that there may not be an immediate return, but recognizing the importance of relationship building and long-term planning. So that foresight, that vision is really paramount. And then this notion also of leveraging existing projects and partnerships, right? So you're saying not to put aside or apart or even feel a way that another group is working on something that you had an intention to do, but leveraging what they have to be a foundation for what the bigger business would do, and creating, again, some additional connections and relationship building within the system, the broader organization system.

How might those who have not yet had an opportunity to come into a system and feel comfortable building those relationships, what are the things that you might suggest that they could do to get that stakeholder engagement and buy-in? Any golden jewels that you can give for folks who are starting to do this work and maybe struggling to get that connection across?

Jaison: So a couple of things, one is at this time, really up until the pandemic started, every Friday at 3:00, or 3:30, Fitbit had happy hour. I always went to the happy hours, particularly my first year. I went to the happy hours all the time unless I was flying back home. You're really hearing what's important. And that's a level of relationship building.

And so I think all of it's harder now. A lot of organizations don't have those types of routines. I would say for me, it's been important to show up and to be a part of routines. And actually, I have a philosophy. And my philosophy is I want to show up as a person, not as a role or a title.

My emails, I don't even have a signature because I just type my initials. That's it. I'm not trying to create layers between you and me. And one of the ways of doing that is also showing up where there are these moments of engagement and relationship building that are ready for you to take advantage of. So that just happened to be one that was right there. And they served dinner and they had free beer, wine, and then some people would bring the stuff I like to drink. Right? But that was one. And I cannot overstate the importance of taking advantage of those types of institutional things that happen, that leaders typically, senior leaders in particular, they'll come and do a drive by. It's not often that they will stay and come back and come back and come back and come back. So that was one. And that was just, I'd say, maybe with the general employee population. And I'll add to that because I still do this to this day.

People go, "I just want to get some time with you. I know you're busy and I'm a..." If I don't meet with you, I'm not doing my job. If I don't make myself available to you, I'm not doing my job. And so I want to make sure that people know. I tell them, "You can Slack me, you can email me. You can just send a note to my admin and say, 'Hey, I need time with Jaison.'" And she knows I'm going to find you time because she knows my philosophy. She's not blocking me from meeting with people. Her job is to help me do that and to manage it so that my life doesn't get out of control.

And I think that's important too, that if you operate as a human and not by level, I think that helps ease the relationship, particularly where there is that dynamic. There isn't organizational hierarchy. Every company has a level of politics. Doesn't mean you have to lean in and lead with that. Right? It can be there and you know it's there, but you don't have to acknowledge it and use that.

The second thing, which I still do now but is not as fun, doing it this way, is I figured out a cadence. And I probably figured out the cadence with my chief people officer. But basically I would try to take the executive team members out for 30 minutes and we'd get coffee. . If it's once every two months, if it's once every six weeks, I felt it was important for me to establish a relationship with every member of the executive team and to have some sort of topic where I wanted to get their input, I wanted to see how they reacted, but I also wanted to give them a forum to go, "Is there anything that you want to share with me?"

And so at Fitbit, that was the thing. I would have an invite to go get coffee. And that paid dividends over time. Not in the same way. I try to meet every six to seven weeks with every member of the executive team.

I do that again as a way just to build a closer connection. And eventually you tend to find out what they are interested in, what they're passionate about. I'll give you another Fitbit example. I got one of my team members. She designed a fantastic program where they went around the world and did all these things. We had, I think after a year, maybe one person had left leadership development.

So many things came from just being able to foster relationships and figure out through conversations where people had interest, passion, and fortunately over time, opportunities came up where we could connect it together.

Another example: the head of product said, "My focus is I want to get more women in product." That became his focus. So the recruiter he worked with found the organization called Women in Product and helped create a relationship between Fitbit and them. And so I'm the diversity guy, also the talent guy. And so they loop me in, invite me to those sessions so I can understand and be part of something that they've initiated, but they're initiating something that was in line with conversations we had.

We wanted to build in more inclusive culture so that we could bring in more diverse talent. When we looked at our diversity data and he looked in product, he's like, "the percent of women here is not where it needs to be. That's going to be my focus area." And it worked out. I didn't need to do much there because John had already committed. He put X amount of dollars, but every time they had a joint event, I was on the invite list, he was there.

But that advanced our inclusion and diversity efforts and enhanced our recruitment efforts because now there was a talent pool that we didn't know existed, called Women in Product, that was very aligned to what he was targeting. But again, it came through relationship and understanding what was important.

And sometimes, to your point around data as the DEI person, I had to come back and go, "Here's the representation of our organization and where do we want to focus? What things do we want to do?" And that just helped with part of that agenda around increasing diversity in our organization, particularly in the tech job families.

Marie: And as you've built those relationships, it paid dividends later for having those invitations now into conversations that helped to kind of connect and build other pieces together. So that's excellent, the sort of deliberate availability. And I also want to underscore this notion of making yourself accessible to folks deeper in the business as a senior leader, not just connecting with folks at your level, but always creating space for people to just take some time on your calendar, which is fantastic. So thanks for sharing that. And how folks can also be thoughtful in creating opportunities to build those connections as well.

In terms of what we've talked about so far, I think I've got a really great sense of where it started, the impetus, some of the key stakeholders, how some of the socialization happened, some of the ways in which you built relationships and established connections. What were the blockers? What were the difficulties that you encountered and how did you overcome them?

Jaison: When we talk about change, there are things that are in your control, there are things that you can influence, and there are things you just have to accept. Right? And while I didn't know those words as a framework or a model at that time, that's probably the way things fell. There were things I had to accept.

So if we talk about diversity in the workforce. When I looked at our US footprint at Fitbit, it was San Francisco, San Diego, and Boston. But when you look overall at the talent pool in California, I mean California as a state is 6 percent Black.

So if you go at a state level, that means you're going from 6 percent—what percent of those are educated, have experience, or are working in fields where we as a tech company would want to recruit them? You're probably already down to 1 percent of native Californians. And super high cost of living. So I remember having a conversation with one of our co-founders like, "Well, how are we going to increase diversity in Boston, San Diego, and San Francisco knowing all this stuff?" It's like, well, we acquired a company in Boston and that's that. Right? And I can't remember how San Diego happened, but he gave me some story and I was like, "Okay, there's nothing changing here. We're not changing location."

So now in 2023, in 2022, everybody's talking about location strategy. When I had these conversations before it was 2000 and I'm going, "Well, I can tell you part of the reason why we don't have diversity. Look where we're located." That conversation with one of the founders let me know you just got to accept that that's not changing. Right? So there were many things that I had to accept that just did not get addressed.

And many I'd say were, I couldn't control them, but I had to influence them. But that influence was over an extended period of time, which means I needed to wait. So while I could tell you in the first three months, I'm like, "This company has no values, we should have company values." I didn't have any organizational support and it was not seen as a priority need for the organization.

I did relationship building. I told people my observations. At some point, all of a sudden now it's important or it's important for a part of the organization and now I have an opportunity to do something about it. So there was a lot more in that influence and needing to wait in order to make something happen.

And then there were things that really just didn't happen. I mean, we never really got a true leadership development curriculum off the ground ahead of both Covid and the subsequent acquisition by Google.

Now, I understood what they were trying to do. They knew whatever. They knew that it was a common practice in tech companies, but that was not something they were willing for us as an organization to do. And so that was an example where it never happened. I couldn't control it, I couldn't influence it. I did the asking. I did everything. Hey, I probably was lucky in the sense that I had the diversity data and I got to have conversations with it explicitly with the executive team, which I guess is good in and of itself, but I wasn't able to go further and to share that externally, which would further have aided in the company's brand.

Marie: I would imagine from your perspective looking at this in a retrospective way, but can you give us a sense of how long it took to go from joining to all of the change that you saw happen? Was all of this embedded prior to your shift into your next role when you left? Give us a sense of how long it took.

Jaison: We created a timeline and the funny thing was the timeline I think started before me and my manager got there.

But I think what we grounded it in was we actually conducted the first engagement survey. So we actually had employee sentiment and data, and that became the anchor. So I would say 2018, all of 2019, all of 2020 was really the journey.

And one of the big things that happened over that period of time for us is we had low scores around senior leaders. I'm trying to see if I can find what the exact set of questions were. But in our engagement survey, it was not really a high score. And over the three years we had a 21-point increase.

A 21-point increase in engagement over the three years. And we also significantly increased the senior leader survey score over that time. So that really showed us that it was working. But again, collective efforts, it wasn't just one thing. It was many things and a lot of it... at the end of the day, culture reflects leadership and vice versa.

And while a lot of this is in hindsight, I do also look at it to go, these are practices that I want to figure out. Like, how do I bring some of those learnings and things forward so then this is atypical of what organizations have experienced? And so how does the atypical become more attainable is what I am hoping to be able to do.

Marie: I have to say the numbers speak volumes. And you anchored the change initially in the employee engagement survey data and you were able to get a very clear measure of accountability and shift with the same or leveraging similar. I know you said you made some changes to the survey itself, but measures of accountability about where you were and where you ended over a course of three years.

And culture change is not easy. Often we're told that it's like trying to turn a giant ship. It takes a long time. But three years for this change. You think that is something that most companies can realistically expect if they were to take similar steps and have similar buy-in to some of what you had going on? Or can they potentially expect something faster depending if they had even more buy-in? What's the realistic scale? Because I'm sure everybody's like, "How long? How long is it going to take to get the change?"

Jaison: Yeah. I would hope that... I mean, three years, I would say if a company is really invested, if I take engagement, that's just a general barometer. I could say you could move 10 points. Right? Now, if you're already at 80, it's probably going to be hard to move to 90. But if you're at 45 or 50, I don't think it's out of the realm of possibility.

One is I made this practice that said... number one, everyone's accountable for engagement, not senior leaders. So I had this one slide that actually said, "Hey manager, here's what your role is in engagement." And I implemented this practice, which was called team fitness. And after every engagement survey, it was very simple. The ask was every manager that gets a report, share your report with your team, set up time to discuss the results with them, and have your team identify the one to two areas that they want to see improved. And manager, it's not your job, number one, to identify the one to two areas. And manager, it is not your job to own and drive the two areas. The team owns it. And your job as a manager is to remove obstacles, help them be successful.

Maybe you are a team member, but you don't have to own it. Right? You need the team to own it and to drive it. I think that was very impactful, especially as it became a rhythm, because I had also changed us to have more frequent pulses in the organization. So we got data too. At one time, we got survey data four times in one year. So that was one thing was everybody has a role.

And so that was the bottom up. If you get every manager doing that as a practice and every team identifies the one or two things that they want to improve for their team, magnify that by how many teams. Now, you also have to have the top down.

So after every survey, or at least once a year, I would present to the company, "Hey…" It was called Fitbit listens. That was how we branded the engagement survey. "Hey, thank you for giving your feedback. We want to create a more engaged team. And based on what we heard from you, these are our three focus areas for the year. And here are the actions that we're going to take in order to make improvements in those areas."

So every time, same folk. Like, "Hey, we heard you, the little whatever up here at the top shifts, what we need in terms of focus area shifts, and then what are the actions we're going to take."

We then had a people and culture goal. So as a company, hey, we want quality products and services that people can't live without. We want to be an integrated health devices company, make our customers healthier. But you know what? We want to be a transparent and engaged team. So it was a longer game. None of this happened in perfect order. The engagement stuff happened before we got a company OKR around people and culture. But that's the other, I call it, trick of the trade. How do you elevate the importance?

And this actually links back to the survey question, you could say. It says, "Senior leaders, VPs, c-level at Fitbit, demonstrate that people are important to the company's success." Well now I've got three business OKRs. And the fourth one is about us: "Build a transparent and engaged team." So now basically you're saying, "The people are as important as the business." And you don't have to go and say, "People are as important as the business. That's why we created this goal." But that's the message it sends.

And so if you are able to articulate that, and then you have some way of saying, "We asked you, we heard you. Here's what we're going to do about it," in a very easy, tangible way. And you get the teams, because this can't be successful top down... so the two things I just talked about were top down. The bottom up is manager, you get a report, share it with your team, have a conversation. Let the team identify the one or two things they want to work on, have a plan around it. You remove barriers, you champion, you do whatever you have to help make those initiatives successful. You keep doing that for 18 months, you're going to have a better organization, right? Because now you've elevated the importance of people and the importance of people is now a conversation that is equally as important as "How's the business performing?"

Marie: And a better example for us to understand what measures of accountability can look like and how it can be developed and integrated, not in a forceful way, but it seems a lot of this was fairly organic, just looking for those plug-in moments. And I love this notion of consistency and driving the cadence over and over again so that folks become familiar. Now it's part of the new piece of what the organization does and how we, in fact, inform what change looks like in the business, which is really fantastic.

Jaison: And one other thing. For people who are in positions of needing to... I don't know if that's the right word, needing to. People who are in positions where they are constantly thinking about assessing the culture and thinking about the possibilities of the culture. That can be anyone. So I don't want to make it, it has to be this person.

One of the things I have learned is that most companies have lookup cultures. So a couple of weeks ago I shared an early version of a talent philosophy with the senior director, leadership development cohort. And in that session, basically it became a focus group, they're giving me feedback. One of the things that came up was they're like, "If Peter and the TLT," which is our executive team, the travel leadership team, "If they did this, if they did that..." And that was the exact same thing that was happening at Fitbit.

At Fitbit, they were like, "If James does this, if Eric does that..." They were the co-founders and exec staff, which was this leadership. "If they do that..." And what I realized is lookup culture is one of the biggest derailers because it's impossible, for a couple of things. One is, every leader is not built to be a charismatic rally cry, get everybody behind them type of person. It's great when you have that, but every leader, that is not their style. They're not going to inspire and motivate you to like, "Oh man, I'm going to rip off my shirt. This is so inspirational." That's one. Two is, anything that flows from the top down takes a really long time because there's umpteen layers in organizations; even small ones probably have more layers than you would like. So in GitHub, let's just say, there's seven to 10 layers. What's it going to take for something to make it through every single layer and for people get on board with it? And so what I have found is in every organization there are leaders who have the title and then there are individual leaders, people who lead themselves. Who are looking up, going, "This would change if they did X." As opposed to going, "What do I control? What do I influence? And what do I have to accept?"

So if you get more people in the organization going, "Man, what do I have control over? The experience of my team. What do I have influence over? The peers that I work with, the way I treat people. What do I have to accept? I got to do performance management. I have to do compliance training." There's certain things you have to accept, but there's more in that grace space of what do I control and what do I influence? And so many people are looking up going, "I need Jamie Dimon to make this decision." No, you don't. In most things, you don't need Jamie or any CEO to make the decision because there's so much about the employee experience that's based off of what happens locally.

So that's one thing people need to understand—if you're look-ing at culture and the examining culture, there tends to be a lot of people who are not prone to take action. They're prone to look up and wait for somebody else to take action. If that doesn't happen, that's their reason for not moving.

The second thing is we become overreliant on the CEO and what message or thing the CEO must do. If it's not in the CEO's wheelhouse, they shouldn't do it, right? Because they can't do it authentically. And Fitbit was really the first place I've ever seen this. So to give you an example, engagement survey data. James, he would talk a little bit to it, but he would either say, "I'm going to hand it over to Lisa," who's the chief people officer, or "I'll hand it over to Jason and they're going to talk about it." Everybody knew it, it wasn't in his wheelhouse. We heap a lot of expectation and assumptions, particularly, on the CEO and the executive team. But it's not always necessary that the CEO and the executive team are the ones that do the stuff.

Marie: The question becomes what happens when they don't buy in? And there is sort of a mismatch between organization data, insights around what needs to happen, leadership sentiments around things being alright, and no real engagement in what actually needs to be different. So if they're not bought in, then what?

Jaison: That's why, going back to the efforts around relationship building, I said at Fitbit, every six or so weeks, I took every execu-tive team member out for coffee. So I, by default, knew the people who were passionate about different areas, and they can represent and influence. It doesn't have to be... so in any executive team there's probably at least one person who does everything I'll say right. Or is a great role model for being a leader who thinks about inclusion, who thinks about developing people. There's probably one person, and they always do it, but the others don't. That one person is your ally. And so you build through those conversations. Again, it doesn't happen all at once, but you build allyship and you help them get what they want and they help you get what you want. And most of the time it's going to be connected.

Marie: And that's such an important piece around grounding in the reality of that nuanced aspect of the relationship building, that allyship connection. Because for many of us in this work, feeling that we have to carry it on our own, but having someone else also being as passionate, with a different level of access and insight, to continue to carry the message forward around what's possible, is such a huge thing.

Jaison: And I would also add, one of the things I personally do is I am a student of... I don't want to say everything culture, but a lot of things culture. So the podcast I was just listening to, walking the dog, "Defining Culture Roadmap." That's what I'm listening to on my podcast, right? Culture roadmap.

I have a picture on my phone that says, "Every day you're not thinking about your culture and being intentional about it, it's inevitable it will become diluted." I have another one, "More stories, less PowerPoint. Practice out loud." I have culture stuff all over. I even have pictures, from CNBC, of companies, how they've been evolving their in-office work requirements. So I have pictures on my phone of what companies have two days in the office, three days, four days or five days. I find it important for me to... I guess as a student of the craft, but as a student of the craft in that I guess it's natural. And at the same time, I'm a student of the business. And so people know I'm always thinking about culture.

Marie: It's not a project, it's a consistent drumbeat. It is the heartbeat of the company that has to remain top of mind so that it doesn't fall through the cracks. You could make all this progress and neglect the core things that help sustain the change or continue to make the evolution even more impactful over time. So I love that notion, just not letting it go off the radar at all, which is fabulous.

Jaison: And so listening to earnings calls, there are people who do that, there are people who don't, who scan the 10K, look at earnings reports.

So then companies like yours, you got the diversity report and everything. So then it's like, "Ah, put it all in one place." But I'm still always interested in how it's represented when companies are reporting earnings because again, that is a reflection of the culture of the company. So again, doesn't always work, doesn't always happen. But those are things for me. One of my biggest aspirations is how has something that I've done show up in the annual report?

Marie: And one of the things we had not yet talked about, that is an area in the book, is this notion of psychological contracts and psychological safety. And to what extent you feel that that has power, significance, and impact on culture transformation work. And what experiences you had around it, either for yourself or for those within the culture transformation experience that you were partnering with.

Jaison: The people on my team who are the OD consultants are working on top team effectiveness, to actually engage with. One of the pivotal focus areas across all of the teams, pretty much, not exclusively but pretty much across all of the teams, is trust and psychological safety. So we recognize it both as something that is an area of opportunity within senior leadership teams, which means it's an area of opportunity in terms of the behavior and the decision-making of individual leaders. Which even if you just add those two things together, that means that there's more than likely—and we have data that says this—but there's a trust deficit across the company and there's a psychological safety deficit as well. That has become more and more important.

I think from my experience, it takes different states and different companies. At Fitbit, we had a whole focus just on allyship. We did whole day things on just how to be an ally. That was the way I think we addressed trust and psychological safety through allyship. Just better understanding the people around you and really taking a broad aperture to trust in psychological safety versus just a narrow one around a person who's physically different than you.

Within Expedia, I think we're probably just understanding what the size of the opportunity is, and we know that if in senior teams that is not happening, then it's going to be very hard for it to happen in the teams that those individuals lead and vice versa.

Instead of saying trust and psychological safety in order to have, it's like psychological safety comes along with trust. I'm calling it out the same. Both of those also have an impact on well-being. The part I put around growth is also there's individual growth, but there's also business growth too. It's a little bit of a play on growth. But I started off to intentionally empower a culture of trust, to highlight the importance and the need for us as an organization to do work in that space. It's very important. Like I said, I think it's different shapes at different companies in terms of how they go after it, just based on their culture and their ways of working. It's important. Also, being able to actually, I don't know if measure's the right word, you can ask a trust question in an engagement survey. You can ask the psychological safety questionnaire. I think that the challenging part is being able to figure out what's the root cause.

Marie: Sometimes the qualitative data, those verbatim statements can help us. I'm not sure how many companies take the time to read thoughtfully through those. It can be many, many statements. The coding that's required. I am a qualitative researcher, so I've done that, hearkening back to my dissertation days around it. But such rich insights, we can get a little bit more about the why.

Which is another thing to potentially look at, but the stats are easier to digest than the verbatim statements. But that aside, one of the last things that I wanted to ask was around self-care. Doing this work is tough, particularly when we are thinking about leaning into what you described around diversity work or even navigating the challenges that come with the blocks and the roadblocks and then the patience that's required. What are some ways that you take to manage the challenges that come with doing this work and maybe even some guidance that you might suggest to those who are embarking on this kind of a journey?

Jaison: Well, there's two parts here. There's what I should do and there's what I do do. What I should do is figure out a day or two per quarter to take off. That's what I should do. That is not the reality. At the same time, I love what I do.

I would encourage people to find their small things, whether it's going out for a walk… I highly encourage my team to log off early. I know you're going to work. I know you're going to do this stuff.

Log off early. I know you'll be killing it the next week. I have a highly motivated and engaged team around the work that they do. But small things. Go for a walk, take walking meetings, which is very hard. I get Zoom and that's become increasingly hard. But we can still go old school. You can call in the Zoom on your phone and you don't have to have video and you can walk. There's other small things I think that people can find that will help them do self-care and well-being with some intentionality.

Marie: When you think back on it all, is there anything that you would've done differently? The culture transformation work at Fitbit?

Jaison: What I would say is what I would've done differently was probably all in my head. I got frustrated at times and I didn't let go of it soon enough. I couldn't always tell you where things were going and if things were working. That can be frustrating because you want to see a material impact in the work that you do, and what do you do when you don't? My current job title has the word culture in it, so I can't hide from it.

At GSK, I was basically hired in to do transformation. A big part of transforming how a business operates is transforming the culture. Well, if they're hiring me and we've got teams working on transformation, obviously they get it. They're not approaching it uninformed.

Leadership's important. Culture means a lot. You got to bring people along.

That business is called Fitbit. It's a very different type of leader to work with. I am now at the point of doing a lot more observation and seeking to understand who is the individual who is CEO than I did prior to my Fitbit experience. Because I didn't understand those things about James. Then understanding that James and Eric created two prior companies with successful exits. James dropped out of

Harvard. That's a different type of phenotype. Different type of persona than what I had been used to. That's important because culture people put an inordinate amount of expectation on the CEO for culture. But if you don't study and understand who the CEO is, you don't really understand what are the elements of culture that individual can help you on and what are the elements of culture it's not for them to help you on, and that's where you need to go. Well, who else can stand in the gap, represent leadership, but talk the talk and walk the walk to help us?

Marie: This sort of postmortem for the Fitbit culture transformation work that you were a part of. Really important reflections. What you shared will be one of the more powerful examples of what can be done in an organization when you've got the right individuals engaged. Not only as participants, but also leading the work. You have the evidence, the data to share what the journey was like.

Jaison: I have one more thing that is actually uber important.

Marie: Yes, please.

Jaison: It happened at Fitbit, and I'm in the pathway of getting this at Expedia. Fitbit was a co-design with my chief people officer. In my opinion, there needs to be a strong, deep alignment with the chief people officer on what you're going after, why you're going after it. For that individual, they're removing obstacles. They are influencing in conversations and spaces where you are not.

Literally, and Lisa would tell you this, she and I would go into a conference room for like three hours and whiteboard a whole bunch of stuff, and we come out with a plan. Basically she'd go, "Jason, that's the plan, go." We co-designed it. The person who hired me at Expedia left about seven months into my tenure. The person who I report to now was not the person who hired me. Maybe that's irrelevant. But one of the things I've been saying to him is, "I want to co-design stuff with you. I want to be able to get in the room and spend time. You and I gonna like, how do we get there? What's your thinking? What's my thinking?"

If you get that, you're not operating on your own. There's a shared agenda and you've got a pact with your head of people. If you're the head of people, maybe you need to do it in reverse, which is who are the people either on your team or in the organization who maybe you need to do that co-designing with?

Not to say that there are not other co-designs, maybe we're co-designing a plan or set of actions, but then there's other co-designing that happens with employees and with other people leaders or leaders in the company to really take it from—we've aligned and strategized on the what and maybe a little bit of the how. But you need those other ambassadors, those other representatives, those other stakeholders to really make the how practical and actionable.

I had my quarterly connect conversation with my manager this morning and he said, "I know you've been asking me for time so we can focus on and do stuff." In the current state, when I worked at Fitbit, I spent a significant amount of time in San Francisco. I was with Lisa. My leader is in New York. Before that my leader was in Chicago, and then my leader travels a lot. It's not as easy as when we were co-located in the same place. But yet still that alignment, that partnership, that shared vision is I think an essential requirement for culture transformation to be successful. Because if you have a chief people officer or CHRO who's not an OD thinker, how do you get to a similar type of outcome?

Marie: Again, that power of the OD framing in this work and the partnership piece is so huge, that co-creation element is such a huge part of that work, such a huge part of the ways in which OD work is done... impossible to get done without it. A critical partner at that in a very specific role. Again, you're highlighting this importance of who's in the rooms that you're not in to continue to carry the work forward. Your chief people officer is indeed a partner that is absolutely required to achieve culture transformation.

Jaison: I guarantee you, Lisa probably had to say something about why it was important for James to be part of creating values for the company. I'm certain that didn't just happen because, oh,

Jaison stumbled upon the engineering team and they're creating their own vibe. I'm certain there was some further conversation that I wasn't privy to that helped gain his buy-in and support to the point where he got up on stage ahead of me, set up the introduction, said this is what they are. Jaison's going to come up here and talk in some more detail to them and what our plan is.

Marie: I would encourage those who are reading this, if you have not gained insight or understanding around OD, I have in other chapters talked about organization development and the ways in which OD work is leveraged for culture change to lean into understanding more about the competencies, but beyond that sort of the overarching inclusive nature of the way OD can help to support culture transformation.

INDEX

Page numbers in *italic* denote a figure or table.

A-LIGN 35
absorption 22
accountability 9, 72, 94, 104, 124, 147,
    155–58, 177, 179–81
action stage (TTM) 95
adaptability 11, 24, 29, 47
Adidas 35
admins (executive assistants) 14, 125, 172
adoption mindset 124
advisory groups 31
advocacy 43–57, 170
affinity groups *see* employee resource groups
    (ERGs)
affordability 25, 40, 41, 54, 141
affordable housing 54, 141
AfroTech 148–49
Age Discrimination in Employment Act
    (1967) 109
'all hands' meetings *see* town hall meetings
allyship 123, 144, 155, 181, 182, 183
    see also relationship building
Amazon 34, 141
Amazon Catalytic Capital 141
Amazon Housing Equity Fund 141
Americans with Disabilities Act (1990) 109
Amnesty International 34
anchors 133–34
annual reports 39, 60, 182–83
Apple 133
application forms 68–69
appraisals 73
appreciative inquiry xiv
Arbery, Ahmaud 152
Argyris, Chris xiii, 5
ASPCA 35
Aspire 36
assistance dogs 39
authenticity 55
AutoDesk 152
awareness 68, 91, 134
AWS Impact Accelerator 141

Bank of America 54
Barbers Hill High School 87–88
barriers *111*, 113–14
    see also resistance to change
Beckhard, Richard xiv, xv
belonging 2, 8, 43–57, 90, 93, 144
    see also employee resource groups
    (ERGs)
Ben & Jerry's 35–36
Ben & Jerry's Foundation 35–36
benefits realization 124
Black Business Accelerator 141
Black representation 65, 87–88, 99–100,
    139, 141–43, 148–49, 174–75
BOKS by Reebok 35
Boston Consulting Group 23–24
Brand, Dalana 151
brand advocacy 43–57, 170
branding 7–8
breach of psychological contract 75–76
Burke, Warner xiv, xv
Burke-Litwin Model xv
Burlington Coat Drive 36
Burlington Stores 36
burnout 147, 148
business, function of 59
business resource groups 143–44, 151
business strategy alignment 147, 149, 150

Call for Code Racial Justice program 53
Cambridge Analytica 71
Camp Skyhook 39
Canine Companions for Independence 39
Capitol riots (2021) 142–43
care 67
CARES Act 33–34
catalysts (employees) 99–117
Catalytic Capital 141
CBRE 36
Center for Creative Leadership 90, 91
certifications xvii

challenger safety 91, 93
change 10, 103–05, 120
    resistance to xvi, 96
    see also barriers
check-ins 30
chief people officers 151, 165, 172, 186–88
chiefs of staff 14, 124–25
Chui, Vanessa 152
Civil Rights Act (1964) 109
Cleveland Clinic 71
climate action 25
climate adaptation 24
climate resilience 24
climate risk 24
co-creation (co-design) 13, 14, 132, 186–87
collaboration 10–11, 120, 171
    see also partnerships
comfort, right to 51
commitment 60, 90
communication xvi, 9, 76, 85, 105–06,
        153–54, 172–73
    see also constructive conversations;
        Courageous Conversations
        program; DEIB conversations;
        emails; interpersonal interactions;
        listening; listening systems; mass
        communication
communities of belonging 144
    see also employee resource groups
        (ERGs)
community outreach 14, 33, 41, 54, 150
compassion 91
compensation 72–73, 77, 94, 151–52
    see also reward systems
conformity 86, 88–89
Constructive Conversation Model 109–10,
        111–12
constructive conversations 31, 82, 109–10,
        111–12
constructive criticism 82, 83
constructive discharge 148
constructive dismissal 147–48
consultancies 132
Consumer Financial Protection Bureau 69
contemplation stage (TTM) 95
continuing education xvii
contracts 59
    see also psychological contracts
contributor safety 91
Corporate Giving Foundation 39–40
corporate lobbying 63
corporate political participation 62–65,
        100–01, 102

Corporate Service Corps 131
corporate social responsibility (CSR) 19–42
cost changes 103, 132
Courageous Conversations program 53–54
covering 55
Covid-19 pandemic 33–35, 36, 60, 61–62
Cox Enterprises 36
cross-border investments 62
crowdsourcing 16, 22
CROWN Act (2019) 87–88
cultural change 103–04, 120
culture 103–04
culture assessments 93

data analytics 24, 46
data breaches 70–71
data privacy 68, 70–71
data protection 68–69
Day of Purpose 37
decision-making 93, 94
dedication 2, 22
defensiveness 51
DEIB 8, 9, 43–57, 93–94, 153
    see also belonging; diversity; equity;
        inclusion
DEIB conversations 49–50
Delivering Good 36
Deloitte 28, 143–44
demographic data 68
Dev Color 170
digital inclusion 34
disability discrimination 109
discomfort 51, 88, 147, 157
discrimination 47, 49, 67, 70, 87–88, 109
disengagement 28, 75–76, 83
    see also employee engagement
Disney 36
diversity 8, 26, 44–57, 65–66, 93, 143–44,
        163, 165–68, 170, 173–76
    failed initiatives 144–49
diversity and inclusion advocates 52
donation matching (fundraising) 22, 23,
        29, 37
DoorDash 152
Dorchester town hall meetings 110
downward power 100
dress codes 87, 88
Drucker, Peter 59

earnings statements 127
economic development 24, 25
Edelman Data x Intelligence 61–62
Edmondson, Amy 9, 81, 82, 86, 96

education sector 25, 36, 39, 40, 41, 99, 108, 130, 175
EEOC 70
emails 171–72
empathy 76, 91, 157
employee advisory groups 31
employee advocacy 43–57, 170
employee catalysts 99–117
employee engagement 2–3, 5–9, 15–17, 19–42, 49–51, 106–15
  see also disengagement
employee engagement surveys 22, 29–31, 50, 55, 66, 164, 168, 169, 176–79, 181, 184
employee experience (social collectives) 8, 14, 126, 128–29, 143, 144, 180
employee forums 30–31
employee health 7, 34, 85
  see also mental health; organizational health; wellbeing (wellness)
employee involvement 23, 26, 28, 32, 44, 169
employee listening systems 50, 107
  see also surveys; town hall meetings
employee partnerships 13–15
employee resource group (ERG) leaders 150–51, 154
employee resource group (ERG) summits 154–55
employee resource groups (ERGs) 3, 14–15, 33, 126, 128, 139–60, 163–64
employee retention (talent retention) 7, 11–12, 49–51, 60, 129, 146
  see also talent management
employee support initiatives 34
  see also flexible working
employer branding 7–8
employment applications 68–69
energy sector 25, 37, 38, 39
engagement 2–3, 5–9, 15–17, 19–42, 49–51, 106–15
  see also disengagement
Engagement Institute 28
engagement surveys 22, 29–31, 50, 55, 66, 164, 168, 169, 176–79, 181, 184
Equal Employment Opportunity Commission 70
equality 24, 25, 130
equity 8, 32, 34–35, 43–57, 72–74, 108
  see also corporate social responsibility (CSR); racial equity (justice)
ERG leaders 150–51, 154
ERG summits 154–55

ERGs 3, 14–15, 33, 126, 128, 139–60, 163–64
Esri 36
EssilorLuxottica 132
ethics xvi–vii, 20, 32, 37, 67, 72, 84, 93
European Union 70
exclusion 8, 48–49, 147
  see also inclusion
executive assistants (admins) 14, 125, 172
executive leaders (teams) 122–23, 172–73
  see also chief people officers; chiefs of staff
exit interviews 31
exit strategies 135–36
external barriers 111
external consultants 132
external partnerships 12–13, 131–33
extrinsic motivation 21, 27–28
eyewear 41, 132

Facebook (Meta) 69, 70–71, 132
facilitators 30, 31, 50, 135, 162, 167
failures (mistakes), learning from 90, 93
fairness 7–8, 21–22, 35, 44, 46–47, 72–74
Fashion Pact 37
Fearless Fund 140
Federal Drug Administration (FDA) 37, 71
Federal Trade Commission 71
feedback 30, 31, 83, 90
  see also constructive criticism
Feeding America 39–40
50/50 Day 167
financial performance 46–47
Fitbit 17, 161–88
F5 Networks 37
Flatiron Health 37
flexibility 6, 11, 44, 60, 77, 86, 96, 120, 134
flexible working 34, 61–62, 77
Floyd, George 65, 152
focus groups 30, 154, 169, 180
  see also facilitators
food systems (security) 23, 24, 34, 39–40
Ford 132
formal office hours 114
fraud 69, 71–72
fundraising (donation matching) 22, 23, 29, 37

Gandhi, Mohandas (Mahatma) 99
gender equality 24, 25, 130
General Motors 132
Generation Z 26
George, Darryl 87–88

Giacalone, Rita 152
GitHub 144, 180
Global Compact 20
global health 24
global partnerships 26
globalization xiv, 20
GO AmeriCorps Fellowship 37
GO Foundation 37
goal setting 28, 73–74, *111*, 158
Goldman Sachs 60
Google 17, 34, 37, 65, 70, 131
    see also Fitbit
Google.org Impact Challenge 131
government interventions 33–34, 35, 63, 64,
    89, 109
graduate programs xvii
Green Machine Campaign 36
group dynamics *see* organizational
    development (OD)
Groupon 37
growth mindset 95–96
GSK 185

hair styles 87–88
Hanson, Teuila 151
'happy hours' 171
healthcare 34, 37, 38, 71–72
Here Matters 41
Herman Miller 37
high-potential programs 67–68
hiring (recruitment) 7–8, 11–12, 65, 67,
    145, 173–74
    see also employment applications
Holmes, Elizabeth 72
Housing Equity Fund 141
human resources function xiv, 126, 127–28,
    153–54
Human Rights Watch 34
humanitarian response 24
hybrid working 60, 61
    see also flexible working

IBM 53, 131
identity alignment 102
IKEA 37–38
Impact Accelerator 141
Impact Accelerator for Women
    Founders 141
imposter syndrome 87
inclusion 14–15, 44–57, 90, 92, 165,
    167–68, 173–74
    digital 34
    ERGs 143–44, 153–56

psychological contracts 65–66, 74–76
psychological safety 89, 93
    see also exclusion
inclusion councils 143–44
inclusion safety 90, 92
individual contributors 125
industry peers 132
influencers 101–03, 115, 129
informal meetings 123, 173
Information Commissioner Office 71
innovation 10, 25, 47–49, 52, 86, 90,
    92, 132
innovation advocates 52
integrity 68–72, 92, 93
Intel 133
inter-organizational partnerships 12–15
internal advocates 51–52
internal barriers *111*
internal partnerships 12–15, 119–31
    see also catalysts (employees); employee
        advisory groups; employee advocacy;
        employee forums; employee
        involvement; employee resource
        groups (ERGs)
international policy 62–65, 100–01, 102
International Society for Organization
    Development and Change
    (ISODC) xvii
internet 34
internships xvii, 54
interpersonal interactions 14, 81, 82, 92,
    102–03
interviews xiv, 31, 88, 113
intrinsic motivation 21, 27, 32, 75
investments 24, 54, 62, 63–64, 141

JLL 38
job security 66–68
Johns Hopkins University 36
Junior Achievement 35
Justice ReMix'd 35

Kalanick, Travis 70
Kim Constructive Conversation
    Model 109–10, *111–12*
King, Dr Martin Luther Jr. 99–100
knowledge-sharing sessions 13–14
Kohl's 38
Kohl's Cares program 38
Kraft Foods 132–33

land use 25
layoffs 103

leadership 14, 28, 69, 76, 83, 84, 94, 96,
        123, 186
    accountability of 156–58, 179–81
    commitment of 155–56
    and DEIB 46–47, 55, 65–66, 147
    ERGs 150–51, 154
    see also Center for Creative Leadership;
        executive leaders (teams); managers;
        top management teams
leadership conferences 14–15
leadership development xiv–v, 46
learner safety 91
learning culture 11, 47
learning management systems
        (LMSs) 169–70
LEGO 38
Let's Play for Change 37–38
Lewin, Kurt xiii
lighting sector 40
limitations 135
LinkedIn 38, 151–52, 170
LinkedIn Learning 170
listening 31, 112, 164
listening systems 49–50, 107
    see also surveys; town hall meetings
lobbying 63
local government agencies 64–65
location strategy 175

maintenance stage (TTM) 95
management by objectives 73–74, 147,
        153, 157
managers 47, 91, 94, 123–24
managing diversity approach 145, 146
marginalized groups 126
mass communication 102
Mayo, Elton xiii
McGregor, Douglas xiii, xv
meaningful work 66
measurement (metrics) 9, 50, 94, 153
meetings 108–09
    informal 123, 173
    one-on-one 30, 114–15
mental health 34, 62, 85
    see also burnout
mentoring 37, 50, 53, 54, 66, 140, 162
Meta (Facebook) 69, 70–71, 132
Microsoft 22, 61–62
middle managers 123–24
Millennials 26
mindset 95–96, 124
mission 26, 28, 36, 48, 68, 70

mistakes (failure), learning from 90, 93
Montgomery bus boycott 99–100
motivation 6–7, 21–26, 75
    extrinsic 27–28
    intrinsic 27, 32
    prosocial 27
Musk, Elon 151
mutual aid networks 34

Nadler, David xiv, xv
names 88–89
NASCOP 37
National Cash Register Company 20
NCI 37
NCR Foundation 38
New Mexico University 54
New York Times Neediest Cases Fund 38
Nike 65
nonprofit organizations 22, 34, 35, 36, 37,
        38, 40, 59, 140
Nordstrom 38–39
NRG 39

Obama, Barack 141–42
offensive material 89
office hours 114
Office of Social Impact 39
one-on-one meetings 30, 114–15
1-1-1 model 131
'one right way' culture 51
open-door policies 30, 105
openness 8, 46–47, 83, 109
organization commitment 60, 90
Organization Development Network
        (ODN) xvii
organizational development (OD) 43, 120
    ethics xvi–vii
    evolution of xiii–iv
    future of xvii–viii
    resistance to xv–vi
    scientific rigor of xvi–vii
organizational health 7, 34, 85
    see also employee health; mental health;
        wellbeing (wellness)
organizational structure 48, 103, 172
outreach programs 14, 33, 41, 54, 150
outside-the-box thinking 93
Owen, Robert 19

Pakistan Women's Empowerment
        Program 35
Panasonic 39, 133

pandemic (Covid-19) 33–35, 36, 60, 61–62
partnerships 12–15, 26, 119–38
    see also catalysts (employees); employee
        advisory groups; employee advocacy;
        employee forums; employee
        involvement; employee resource
        groups (ERGs)
passion 182
Patagonia 39
paternalism 51
Patterson, John H. 20
peer-to-peer feedback 31
PepsiCo 64
performance 7
performance appraisals 73
performance management 46–47, 48, 94,
    163–66, 169–70
performance ratings 166
personal anchors 133–34
personality tests xvi
PetSmart 39
PetSmart Paws for Hope 39
Philanthropy Cloud 39
planned change paradigm xiv
politics 62–65, 100–01, 102
power (power market) 100–01
power hoarding 51, 147–48, 156
power sharing 157
precontemplation stage (TTM) 95
preferred names 88–89
preparation stage (TTM) 95
Pride ERG 163, 166
problem-solving 47–49, 85–86, 156
process changes 103
process consultation xv
Procter & Gamble 53–54
production 25
productivity 7
professional development xvii, 31, 66, 155
progress updates 29
pronouns 88–89
prosocial motivation 27
prototypical culture 103–04
psychological availability 16
psychological comfort 51
psychological contracts 2, 5–9, 59–79,
    183–84
psychological safety (safe spaces) 2, 9–12,
    81–98, 107–10, 148–49, 183–84
public goal setting 158
pulse surveys 22, 31, 168
purpose 2

Q&A sessions 113
qualitative research 184
quiet firing (quitting) 60

RACI chart 119–20
    see also accountability
'Racial Equality and Economic Opportunity'
    (BOA) 54
racial equity (justice) 65, 140, 141–43,
    147, 152
'Racial Equity Action and Change'
    (Target) 54
Ray-Ban 132
reactive behaviour 134–35
readiness for change 43, 104–05
Reboot Representation Tech
    Coalition 53–54
recruitment (hiring) 7–8, 11–12, 65, 67,
    145, 173–74
    see also application forms
reductions in force 103
reflection 112
regulators 62, 63, 71, 132
relationship building 121–22, 175, 181
    see also allyship
remote working 60
REP 38
reporting 39, 60, 177, 182–83
resilience 11, 24, 83, 92–94
resistance to change xvi, 96, 104–05
    see also barriers
resource, defined 144
respect 49, 74–76, 89, 93
responses 112
return on investment (ROI) 124
reward systems 28, 69, 73, 147, 150–52
    see also compensation
risk taking 46, 90
role modelling 181
roundtables 50

safe spaces (psychological safety) 2, 9–12,
    81–98, 107–10, 148–49, 183–84
Safeway 71
Saint John, Bozoma 70
salaries 73
sales teams 127
Salesforce 39, 131
Salt March (Satyagraha) 99
scapegoating 51, 147, 157
Schein, Edgar xiii, xiv, xv
School Nutrition Foundation 39–40

Schwan's Food Company 39–40
SDGs 24–26
secretaries *see* executive assistants (admins)
Securities and Exchange Commission 69,
    71, 72
self-awareness 68, 91, 134
senior leaders 123
    see also executive leaders (teams)
shared values 8, 104
sideways power 100
Signify 40
Signify Foundation 40
social accountability 156, 158
social change (impact) 23–33, 36, 62–65,
    130–31
social collectives (employee experience) 8,
    14, 126, 128–29, 143, 144, 180
social equity 8, 32, 34–35, 43–57,
    72–74, 108
    see also corporate social responsibility
    (CSR); racial equity (justice)
Social Impact Accelerator 36
Social Impact Institute 24–26
social impact services 23–24
social interactions 128–29
social media 70–71, 85, 101
    see also Facebook (Meta); LinkedIn;
    Twitter
Solomon, David 60
SOS Children's Village 35
South by Southwest Festival 70
Southwire 40
specialized teams 14
sponsorship 50, 53, 153, 164, 167, 169
stakeholder theory 20
stakeholders 20, 119–38
    engagement with 171–74
    identification of 12–13, 14
Starbucks 132–33
startups 36, 71–72, 124, 141, 163
strategy xiv–v, 135–36, 147, 149, 150, 175
Strivers Grant Contest 140
Students 2 Science Newark Technology
    Center 39
Success Academy 40
surveys 107
    engagement 22, 29–31, 50, 55, 66, 164,
        168, 169, 176–79, 181, 184
    pulse 22, 31, 168
sustainability 23–26, 36, 37–38, 39,
    40, 64, 131
sustainability advocates 52
Sustainable Development Goals 24–26
sustainable finance 24

Sustainable Living Plan 131
Sustainable Style 37
Synovus 40–41

talent management 46, 66–68, 84, 150
talent retention (employee retention) 7,
    11–12, 49–51, 60, 129, 146
Target Corporation 54, 65
Target Scholars 54
Target Scholars Sophomore Internship 54
target setting 46
team-building xiv, 85–86, 92, 145
techno-structural interventions xiv
technology xiv, xviii, 36–37, 53–54
    see also internet
Techstars 36
Tesla 133
Theranos 71–72
Thomson Reuters 24–26
360-degree feedback 30
top management teams 13, 106
    see also leadership
town hall meetings 30–31, 110, 112–14
training and development 31, 50
trans communities 153–54
transparency 9, 30, 45, 47, 48, 72, 73, 92
Transtheoretical Model 95–96
triggers 134–35
trust xvi, 8, 10–11, 30, 50, 68–72, 76,
    101–02, 184
Twitter 151

Uber 69, 70
UNICEF 37
uniformity 88–89
Unilever 131
United Nations 20, 24–26
United Negro College Fund 54
United States Congress 71
United States Justice Department 69
United States Supreme Court 100, 140
unspoken (unwritten) employee
    expectations 59, 61–76
upward power 100

values 8, 74, 104, *111–12*, 134, 164,
    170, 175
values alignment 60
Virtual Volunteer Week 37
volunteering 28, 29, 35, 37, 41, 130,
    140, 150
vulnerability 91

Warby Parker 41

water resources 25, 64
wellbeing (wellness) 52, 62
    see also employee health; mental health;
        organizational health
wellness advocates 52
Wells Fargo 69
'what's in it for me?' 156
White response, to diversity 48–49
White supremacy culture 51, 147
WiAM 38
Williams, Jaison 16–17, 161–88
Women in Product 173
wording 112
work-life balance 61–62, 185
Work Trend Index 61–62

Workday Learning 169–70
workplace harassment 70, 89, 109
workshops 13–14
World Wildlife Fund 38
'worth it' equation 61–62

Xerox National Black Employees
    Caucus 139

young employees 62
    see also Generation Z; Millennials

zero-tolerance policies 47
Zoom meetings 114, 185
Zuckerberg, Mark 71

Looking for another book?

Explore our award-winning
books from global business
experts in Human Resources,
Learning and Development

Scan the code to browse

www.koganpage.com/hr-learning-
development

Also from Kogan Page

ISBN: 9781398615496

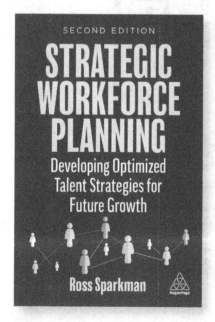

ISBN: 9781398607279

ISBN: 9781398612594

www.koganpage.com

Printed in the USA
CPSIA information can be obtained
at www.ICGtesting.com
JSHW011518260524
63706JS00003B/11